An Emerging Woman

alba house ▪ DIVISION OF THE SOCIETY OF ST. PAUL
STATEN ISLAND, N. Y. 10314

an

♥EMERGING

♥WOMAN

S. Therese Catherine, O.P.

Nihil Obstat:
    William F. Hughes
    Censor Deputatus

Imprimatur:
    Walter P. Kellenberg, D.D.
    Bishop of Rockville Centre
    June 2, 1970

The nihil obstat and imprimatur are official declarations that a book or pamphlet
is free of doctrinal or moral error. No implication is contained therein that those who
have granted the nihil obstat and imprimatur agree with the contents, opinions or
statements expressed.

Library of Congress Catalog Card Number: 71-129172

SBN: 8189-0190-X

Designed, printed and bound in the U.S.A. by the Pauline Fathers and Brothers of
the Society of St. Paul, 2187 Victory Blvd., Staten Island, N.Y. 10314 as part of their
communications apostolate.

IN LOVING MEMORY
OF

Rt. Rev. Msgr. John A. Cass
because of whose interest
in the Amityville Dominicans
this book
was written

The upper left portion of the shield signifies the origin of the Congregation. The eagle is an emblem of Bavaria in which Ratisbon is located. The cross at the lower left signifies the Order of Preachers. The Marian symbol at the upper right indicates the title and patron of the Motherhouse. The M A is for Mary, and the crown honors her as Queen of the Rosary. At the lower right, the three gold roses of four petals each signify the twelve Congregations which grew from the parent Community at Ratisbon, Bavaria.

The motto, Veritas, Truth, is that of the Dominican Order.

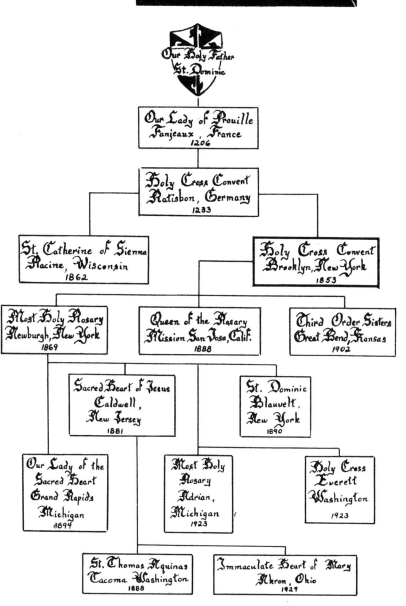

Tracing Our Lineage . . .

Our Holy Father
St. Dominic

Our Lady of Prouille
Fanjeaux, France
1206

Holy Cross Convent
Ratisbon, Germany
1233

St. Catherine of Sienna
Racine, Wisconsin
1862

Holy Cross Convent
Brooklyn, New York
1853

Most Holy Rosary
Newburgh, New York
1869

Queen of the Rosary
Mission San Jose, Calif.
1888

Third Order Sisters
Great Bend, Kansas
1902

Sacred Heart of Jesus
Caldwell, New Jersey
1881

St. Dominic
Blauvelt, New York
1890

Our Lady of the
Sacred Heart
Grand Rapids
Michigan
1894

Most Holy
Rosary
Adrian,
Michigan
1923

Holy Cross
Everett
Washington
1923

St. Thomas Aquinas
Tacoma Washington
1888

Immaculate Heart of Mary
Akron, Ohio
1929

FOREWORD

Dominican religious are today living in an era which tends to test their traditional loyalty to the Church. History will no doubt show that they have not been found wanting. If so, much of this renewed love of the Spouse of Christ will have been enkindled by efforts to re-live the spirit of Saint Dominic, to determine how he would have faced the problems which beset us today, and to attack them under the impulse of this renewal.

Our Dominican Sisters are more than ever eager to manifest this spirit. Not only have they the example of Saint Dominic but they are also inspired by the special aim and ideals of the saintly Foundresses of their Congregations.

Sister Therese Catherine has endeavored to re-present the spirit and aims of Mother M. Josepha in the hope that "her daughters may find courage to pursue the renewal of their religious commitment in her spirit."

This work seems to me to be truly in the spirit of

the Church's desires for all Institutes, and should greatly contribute to the genuine renewal of the large community of Amityville Sisters. I feel sure also that other Congregations will share the benefits of this research, especially those who owe their foundation, directly or indirectly, to Mother Mary Josepha. I heartily bless the efforts of all her daughters to spread the truth of the Gospel with renewed intensity in the recaptured spirit of Saint Dominic and their self-effacing yet most energetic Foundress.

Fr. Aniceto Fernandez, O.P.
Master General

Rome, Santa Sabina, January 10, 1970

PREFACE

For one hundred and sixteen years, the Sisters of St. Dominic who came from Ratisbon, Bavaria, have labored to gather in the rich harvest of souls on Long Island. Their story is traced through the difficult pioneering days into the rich garnering of the mid twentieth century by Rt. Rev. Msgr. Eugene J. Crawford in "The Daughters of Dominic on Long Island."

During this recital of heroic deeds and amazing sacrifices, a woman, whom thousands of Dominican Sisters salute, directly or indirectly, as "Foundress," remained a shadowy outline slipping in and out of the pages of a Community's history. That woman, the noble woman of faith, Mother M. Josepha Witzlhofer, has intrigued the author for many years.

In an effort to fill in the shadowy outline with flesh and blood, nerve and sinew, emotions and character, the author searched archives in the Motherhouses of Ratisbon and Amityville as well as in the city archives of Regensburg. She has read accounts of foundations springing from Ratisbon and Williamsburg. Too, a study was made of the environmental background of Germany and America which might throw the woman, Maria Teresa Witzlhofer, into relief.

The result is, the writer trusts, the life of a woman emerging from cold statistics and historical data into a real person to be loved and venerated.

In the Vatican Council decree, "Perfectae Caritatis," the Bishops of the world urged:

"In order that the great value of a life consecrated by the profession of the counsels and its necessary mission today may yield greater good to the Church, the sacred synod lays down the following prescriptions.

The adaptation and renewal of religious life includes both the constant return to the sources of all Christian life and to the original spirit of the institutes and their adaptation to the changed conditions of our times. This renewal under the inspiration of the Holy Spirit and the guidance of the Church, must be advanced according to the following principles:

a) Since the ultimate norm of the religious life is the following of Christ set forth in the Gospels, let this be held by all institutes as the highest rule.

b) It redounds to the good of the Church that institutes have their own particular characteristics and work. Therefore, let their founders' spirit and special aims they set before them as well as their sound traditions — all of which make up the patrimony of each institute — be faithfully held in honor."[1]

In obedience to the command of the Church "let their founders' spirit and special aims . . . be faithfully held in honor," this author has endeavored to bring to the fore the spirit and aims of Mother M. Josepha so that her daughters may find courage to pursue the renewal of their religious commitment in her spirit. This little book should come to all Dominicans as a response, at least indirectly, then, to the call of Vatican II. For here was a woman whose appeal should reach out to all enthusiasts for change. Here was a woman interested in true reform; in change that would ensure personal and community progress; in search for the deepening of charity.

Finally to the words of Msgr. Crawford, "Are we forgetting the prayers and sufferings of Mother Josepha in our summary of the causes of this tremendous increase, the beginning of a steady enlargement of the Community,"[2] we reply with an effort to remember the woman — her work, her sacrifices, and above all, her pangs as she gave birth to the Congregation of the Holy Cross, the Congregation that salutes her proudly as "Foundress."

The author owes a serious debt of gratitude to the

1. Gonzales, Rev. J. L., S.S.P., (Comp.), *The Sixteen Documents of Vatican II* (Boston), p. 300.
2. Crawford, Rt. Rev. Eugene J., *Daughters of Dominic on Long Island* (Benziger, 1937), p. 96.

present Prioress of Holy Cross, Mother M. Amanda, O.P. and her Community-for their loving interest and invaluable assistance in searching for pertinent material in the archives. Also, thanks is due to Mr. Raymond Sterl who during the author's visit to the archives of the city of Regensburg and since, has continued to offer whatever information was available for the completion of the biography.

Several volumes have been written from which the author has gleaned material. She wishes, therefore, to thank Rt. Rev. Eugene J. Crawford, Sister Hortense Koehler, O.P., Christine Sevier, and Katherine Burton for permission to quote from their works.

An Emerging Woman

CHAPTER I

"Unless the grain of wheat falls into the ground and dies, it remains alone. But if it dies, it brings forth much fruit." (John 12:25, 27)

The day dawned brightly over the bustling town of Williamsburg. The sun stealthily slipped into the tiny sick room of Holy Cross Convent to rest lovingly on the wasted, drawn features of the woman whom Divine Providence had marked as the Foundress of the Brooklyn Sisters of St. Dominic. It was April 9, 1864.

Slowly, the pain-filled eyes of Mother Josepha opened to fix a tender glance on the Crucified above her bed. Her whole being yearned for release — release from the long rendezvous with fever and the unrelenting struggle for breath these long, weary months — release from the overwhelming sense of failure that had enveloped her these last few weeks. He, too, had tasted the bitter gall of strenuous effort with little to show. Calvary's height caught the shadow of only three faithful followers, a pitiful showing for One Who over the past three years had held thousands spellbound. And Mother Josepha had so little to show after ten years of tilling the soil to bring to full growth the transplanted seeds from her dear Ratisbon.

Her mind's eye turned back to that early morning of July 25, 1853, when with a heart torn between apostolic enthusiasm for the beckoning fields of America, white for the harvest, and the wrenching of precious ties with the loved Motherhouse of Holy Cross, she stepped on the gangplank of the "Germania." How her heart yearned to share her own burning love of God with the unspoiled hearts of America's children. She stood resolutely facing the far-distant Bavarian hills, remembering with a shudder the sickening journey from "there" to "here." Her delicate constitution paid a high price for such a trip and the long sleepless nights conjured up terrifying doubts about the whole venture. "Why not return to the tranquil security of Holy Cross and let the more robust take on the task of carrying Dominic's torch to the far-distant shores?" Only her indomitable courage and trusting faith hushed the recurring taunt. And now, here she was, weak but resolute, ready to sail into the unknown while releasing her hold on the cherished familiar.

Her dying gaze left the crucifix as the door of the room softly opened. Silhouetted against the shadow outside, stood her faithful companion, Sister Seraphine, into whose capable hands Mother Josepha had willingly slipped the reigns of government several years before. Gently, ever so gently, her Superior moistened the parched lips of Mother Josepha, the while whispering the sacred names of Jesus and Mary — Jesus who stood just beyond the almost transparent veil waiting, and Mary, "the clement, the loving, the sweet Virgin," whom Mother's lovely voice had invoked every night, "to show unto us the blessed fruit of your womb."

A shadow crossed the face of Mother Josepha. Dying is no simple thing although we die a bit each day. Satan, "the roaring lion prowling about seeking someone to devour," had no intention of permitting this prize to slip through his greedy grasp without a final struggle. He played his trump card! A loyal daughter, trained to respect and reverence God's authority vested in His Church, Mother Josepha had to all appearances violated a serious rule of the Order, a rule which decreed that any Sister who erected a new convent without the consent of the General Chapter and of the Bishop of that diocese in which the convent was to be founded was excommunicated. "What about St. Nicholas Convent on Second Street?" he asked triumphantly. How dare she presume to appear for judgment with the weight of that act of pride tilting the scales against her.

To the eyes of Sister Seraphine and the small band of Sisters gathered in the sick chamber some glimpse was given of the violent spiritual struggle going on in the contorted face of their dying Foundress. Suddenly, the air vibrated with the sweet strains of the "Salve Regina"—"Hail, holy Queen, Mother of Mercy, hail our life, our sweetness, and our hope." Yes, our hope! Mother Josepha's ear caught the word and clung to it with all the strength of her noble soul. Was she not a daughter of Dominic, "the Athlete of the Lord"? Had not Mary herself shown Dominic the chosen spot for his children under her mantle? Had not her own fingers caressed the rosary daily as she pleaded, "Pray for us now and at the hour of our death"?

Gradually, the features relaxed, her usual serenity returned; peace and joy mingled in the dying eyes of this valiant woman. The seed, chosen by God to rest in alien soil, was ready to be plowed under. Mother Josepha was dead!

CHAPTER II

"Unless the Lord build the house they
labor in vain who build it."
(Psalm 126:1)

Regensburg, a city of seven names, dates back
3,000 years and rests at the most northerly point of
the largest river of Europe. It has been in turn, a
Celtic settlement (hence the more ancient name, Ratisbon), the Roman stronghold of "Castra Regina,"
the capital of Bavaria, a ducal, regal and episcopal
city at one and the same time, a world-famous com-
mercial city in the early Middle Ages, a free Imperial
City. Emperors and Kings, saints and scholars, have
left their mark on the city. Albertus Magnus ruled
the ancient diocese under whose tutelage the Angel
of Schools, St. Thomas Aquinas, was to blossom into
the most renowned of the Church's theologians.

Perhaps one of the most remarkable achievements
of this ancient city has been its ability to preserve

the heritage from its great past. As Christine Sevier says in "From Ratisbon Cloisters":

"The early chronicles of Ratisbon tend to stir the deepest enthusiasm of the Christian scholar. The dauntless bishops and heroic saints venerated through the centuries in this Bavarian town, have individually absorbed and emphasized all the inflexibility of purpose and indomitable courage of the stern Roman conquerors. Emmeran, Wolfgang, Ruppert and their co-workers, were cast in colossal mold, supreme exemplars of burning zeal, high courage and lofty consecration. Impenetrable forests held no terrors for these ambassadors of Christ, neither could flood or torment halt them, or the threats of barbarious natives force them to cringe or cower. Their names are shrined in the heart of the nation, to whom their deeds are household tales, told and retold when the fires burn low and the tired children cling to their elders. Under the influence of this hallowed folklore the veil is lifted from a distant age, and the land appears saint-infected, drenched with the blood of martyrs, spilt for the flowering of the Gospel message."[1]

This is the city which Mother Josepha called her birthplace.

---

1. Sevier, Christine, *From Ratisbon Cloisters* (Privately printed, 1917), p. 17.

Maria Teresa was born at ten o'clock in the morning of September 20, 1817, the sixth child of Simon Witzlhofer and Catherine Wilhelm, and was baptized the following day in the cathedral of Niedermunster. A carpenter friend's wife, Magdalena Schmalzl, was her sponsor.

Little Maria Teresa was to know her father briefly, for Simon Witzlhofer died October 17, 1823 when she was six and her mother Catherine had to face the future with eight fatherless children, the oldest, Anna Maria, eighteen, and the youngest, Aloysia, a baby in arms. The seed does not fall far from the tree. In the difficult days ahead, Maria Teresa learned at first hand how a truly Christian woman of faith meets and is molded by the cross. In the shadow of that same cross, the future Foundress of the Holy Cross Congregation cultivated the traits of character demanded of one whom Divine Providence marked for a cross bearer.

Simon Witzlhofer as far as can be determined from the archives of the city had moved into Regensburg from Schwabelweis, a small town twelve miles outside the city walls. He was a game warden and had married Catherine Wilhelm, a farmer's daughter from Nedergebraching. The family had rented rooms at F158 and H145 neither of which exists today. At Simon's death Maria Teresa had begun her education at the convent school of the Dominican Sisters of Holy Cross.

The convent school has a very interesting history. In 1237, sixteen years after the death of our Holy

Father, St. Dominic, Holy Cross Convent was opened. That it was the first Dominican Convent on German soil could be disputed. Evidently, the acceptance of the Rule of St. Sixtus and the approval of Bishop Siegfried for the convent dates from February 22, 1233, a year before the establishment of St. Mark's at Strassburg. Whether first or third to be founded in Germany, it was the only Dominican convent to "weather the storms of persecution, revolution and decay and to enter upon the twentieth century with a flawless, vigorous continuity."[2]

However, this is not to imply that the Regensburg convent was left unscarred by the ravages of the centuries. It, like all the religious houses in Europe in general, and of Germany in particular, tottered on the brink of destruction at various periods of its history. Any number of factors contributed to this.

Between 1348 and 1350 the devastating plague that swept over all of Europe decimated not only cities but Monasteries as well. German religious deaths reached the staggering total of 124,000. Holy Cross was not passed over by the avenging Angel of Death. The diminishing of its ranks resulted in a decadence of discipline which was restored only through the efforts of Bl. Henry Suso, Bl. Raymond of Capua, Master General, and Bl. Conrad of Prussia.

Two centuries later, reformed Regensburg was again

---

2. Kohler, Sister Mary Hortense, O.P., *Life and Work of Mother Benedicta Bauer* (Bruce, 1937), p. 6.

threatened. But this was a far more subtle attack. It came in the form of harrassing persecution following the brazen tacking of his 95 theses on the cathedral doors of Wittenburg by Martin Luther. As the Protestant Revolt spread through Germany, religious women in particular were the target of the reformers.

> "Return to the world and marry"—was the content of the advice given by ministers of the new teaching to the poor Sisters. The procedure against them was generally the following: First, the confessor was removed by force, if he had not already apostatized. A Protestant preacher was placed in the convent in his stead; with the intention of forcing the Sisters to adopt the new religion, they were compelled to attend lectures given by the heretics. Every Catholic service was forbidden. The administration of the sacraments was impossible unless a priest in disguise or under the cover of darkness could bring the comforts of religion to the suffering inmates. All tokens of the old faith disappeared. Books, pictures, water fonts,—all were removed—and often they were destroyed with much vandalism."[3]

Wars play havoc in any generation and Holy Cross Convent knew the terrors of armed conflict long be-

---

3. Wilms, H., *Geschichte der deutschen Dominikanerinnen*, p. 197. Or Hortense, p. 22.

fore a bomb found its target through its roof in World War II. Beginning with the Thirty Years War (1618-1648) and culminating in the Napoleonic invasion with its resulting secularization of religious houses, the Nuns of Regensburg knew the pinch of poverty, the fear of violated enclosure, the piling up of debts of seeming insurmountable proportions.

Finally, as mentioned above, came the threat of secularization. Of all the Dominican Convents in Germany, Holy Cross alone was to escape and remain standing during the unbelievable catastrophe that struck at the Sisterhoods everywhere in Germany. With the destruction of the German Empire, came the seizure of Church property by the princes in compensation for confiscation of their possessions. During the reign of Maximilian IV, 400 convents were closed or despoiled and the Sisters either sent back into the world or herded like cattle into a central convent with a pittance of a pension on which it was all but impossible to subsist.

And Holy Cross? They were prepared for the worst when in 1803 a commissary entered the convent to ask each individual Sister to choose between returning to the world with a pension or remaining in the convent. Today, when returning to the world seems the "right" thing to do, we might look at the courageous Sisters of our past as they spurned the offer of supposed "freedom" and remained loyal to the heritage so faithfully cherished for over six centuries. But they stayed at a price! "Take charge of the schools in the city, or be suppressed," was the order issued by the Prince-Bishop Dalberg. It brought consternation to the Sisters. How reconcile the life of contemplation hitherto led by them with the drastic innovation the assumption of educating the young would necessitate? What about enclosure?

In a show of authority, the prince-bishop angered by the Sisters' resistance, arranged suitable rooms for classes within the enclosure, a faculty was prepared, and the school was opened. It was here in 1823 that Maria Teresa Witzlhofer was sent to be molded mentally and spiritually by these true daughters of Dominic.

The course of study pursued by Maria Teresa included: Religion, German, Mathematics, possibly Latin, very fine needlework and Music. The latter subject was exceptionally important at that time and in a city renowned as the home of the well-known "Domspatatzen," the boys' choir of Regensburg Cathedral. Music was in the very air and Maria Teresa was a real daughter of her native soil. In the school records extant at the ancient Holy Cross Convent, Maria Teresa's rating for music was "Excellent."

As day by day the young girl observed the radiant joy of her beloved teachers, she must have guessed something of the source of that "other-world" radiance surrounding the Sisters who taught. One of these was the future Mother Prioress, Mother Benedicta Bauer, who would play such a striking part in the life of the young student at her feet.

What secret spiritual well did these women drink from behind those mysterious cloistered walls? How

Maria Teresa's receptive, sensitive nature absorbed the wealth of noble example surrounding her. The soil was readying for the seed and Maria Teresa confided her desire to be a follower of Dominic to one of the Sisters.

Holy Cross Convent welcomed its eager candidate on March 9, 1838. She was twenty years of age, tall and willowy in appearance, with a keen mind ready to place her talents at the disposal of Mother Hyacintha, the ruling Prioress.

CHAPTER III

"Arise my love, my dove, my beautiful
one and come."
(Cant. of Cant. 2:10-11)

Note was made in the previous chapter concerning the phases of deterioration and restoration through
which Holy Cross Convent had passed during its long
history. What, one may ask, was the spiritual and physical condition of the community when the youthful
Maria Teresa Witzlhofer stepped across the threshold
separating her from the outside world in 1838?

Mother Benedicta Bauer, only seven years after
Maria Teresa began her religious life, found herself
faced with the difficult and normally thankless task
of restoring religious discipline to Holy Cross. Are
we to conclude, then, that all was in perfect order
when the young postulant began her climb up the
arduous road to perfection? Did she find that religious
life within the cloister corresponded completely with
the image she had formed from her association with

the Sisters over the years of her childhood and ado-
lescence?

A brief look at the account of Sister Mary Hortense Kohler's life of Mother Benedicta Bauer during
the period of 1838 to 1845 reveals a religious house
gradually but not completely recovering from the in-
roads of the secularization following the Napoleonic
Wars. Says Sister Hortense:

> "The Monastic door that closed the world to Maria
> Anna Bauer on July 2, 1820, ushered her into a
> rather unsettled religious readjustment after the
> troublous political upheaval caused by the Napo-
> lenic Wars. . . ."

She continues:

> "It is impossible to gauge just how far religious
> discipline had relaxed, or in what state of deca-
> dence the youthful aspirant found the convent."[1]

From another source closer to home, Msgr. Eugene
J. Crawford in his "Daughters of Dominic on Long
Island," we learn that:

> "During the years of Sister Benedicta's teaching ca-
> reer, the discipline of the Community gradually
> lapsed until it was in a state of deterioration. Sister

---

1. Kohler, Sister Mary Hortense, O.P., *Life and Work of
Mother Benedicta Bauer* (Bruce, 1937), p. 42.

Benedicta experienced in her daily life the confusion, laxity, restlessness of spirit among the Sisters, which are the unhappy counterpart of convent life when superiors are too weak to exercise vigilance or subjects are too self-willed and worldly to submit to direction."[2]

Since Mother Benedicta Bauer was not elected Prioress until 1845, we have every reason to assume that the atmosphere described above prevailed when Maria Teresa began her postulancy.

From an almost superficial study of the psychology of the "person," especially of the young female "person," it is not too difficult to determine the impact that "confusion, laxity, and restlessness of spirit among the Sisters" must have had on one who sincerely sought and expected to find a well-ordered religious life. One need only look at its counterpart in religious communities today, where a century later, the same "confusion and restlessness of spirit" coupled with "superiors too weak to exercise vigilance or subjects too self-willed and worldly to submit to direction," to understand even in small measure the problems Maria Teresa encountered.

However, in the companionship of women like Sister Benedicta and a few others of like aspirations, the young vocation matured into a vigorous, strong conviction that God had work for her to do. For within four months of her entrance we find the fol-

---

2. *Op. cit.,* p. 35.

lowing statement of her clothing in the Archives of
the Community Motherhouse:

> "As we have already given permission six months
> ago to admit Teresa Witzlhofer to the enclosure
> as a candidate for the Order and it has been
> proved that she possesses all the qualifications re-
> quired for the reception of the habit, we declare
> that the Ordinary has no reason to deny the peti-
> tion of Mother Prioress to invest said candidate
> with the habit of the Order."
> Ratisbon, July 13, 1838.

B. Urban, V.G.
Bauernfeld, Sec.[3]

What were *all the qualifications* the now Sister M.
Josepha possessed to which the document above re-
fers? St. Thomas Aquinas, her Dominican Brother, has
insisted that "grace builds on nature," and nature ma-
tures, like grace, gradually and almost imperceptibly.
That being so, the mature years of Mother Josepha
attested to some of the fine qualities the Community
recognized in the young aspirant. Among them was
flexibility, so transparently clear in her decisions
while Superior of the American foundation—a flexibility imperative in one so violently uprooted from the
well-structured, smoothly-regular life of a cloistered
life of a Dominican and plunged into the swirling

---

3. *Archives,* Holy Cross Convent, Amityville. Or Crawford,
p. 99.

vortex of a young vigorous country flexing its muscles and demanding of all, religious and secular alike, a fine balance to weld the old with the new and produce the masterpiece of Catholicity so much the envy of the old world.

Too, there must have been fructifying in the soul of the future pioneer of two Dominican foundations, that rare quality of common sense which the great Carmelite reformer and foundress, Mother Teresa of Jesus, found more important in her subjects than any other virtue.

Finally, there is that splendid attribute without which one in a position of authority finds it impossible to govern successfully—the gift of understanding. In a letter from Regensburg dated August 20, 1962, Sister M. Theresia Graf, O.P., Sub-Prioress of Holy Cross wrote to the author:

> "The first Superior in the new convent was Sister M. Josepha Witzlhofer. She was a very *understanding, wise,* and *pious* woman who well understood how to take care of a house, how to make use of opportunities together with *good common sense,* so that one could hardly find a more fitting person for this new foundation."

On this solid foundation, Sister M. Josepha began her novice year of in-depth religious formation. The young woman drank deeply of the rich tradition of the Dominican Order. She learned to love and venerate the "Watchdog of the Lord," the strong but gentle Saint who "spoke only of God or to God." By a study of the history of the Order, she imbibed as an infant at its mother's breast, the spirit of her founder —the courage that begged of his would-be murderers:

> "I know I am unworthy of the grace of martyrdom but if God in His mercy would grant me this privilege, I would beg you not to kill me at once but to tear me limb from limb, to make my martyrdom a slow one so that hardly human in form, blinded and one mass of blood, I might suffer the extremity of pain to reach a much higher place in heaven."[4]

the joyous spirit that sang lustily as he traversed the lanes of southern France, encouraging his footsore, weary band to rejoice in the privilege of suffering for the Gospel; the tender, childlike love for the lovely Queen Mother at whose command Dominic founded the Order.

Is it any wonder, then, that Sister M. Josepha yearned to be a full-fledged daughter of such a Father. She asked for the privilege of professing her vows. On August 20, 1839 that request was granted:

> "In consideration of the Certificate of Birth of the novice in question and because of her model behavior during the one and a half years that Teresa

---

4. Dafrose, Mother M., O.P., *Fifteen Tuesdays in Honor of St. Dominic* (Brooklyn, 1944), p. 4.

Witzlhofer was in the Novitiate; and having complied with the laws of the State regarding the age, 21 years, the Ordinary has no objection to her being admitted to the first profession for three years."

August 20, 1839   B. Urban, V.G.
                                   Baurenfeld, Sec.[5]

What were the emotions surging through the white-veiled novice as she stepped from the large room on the morning of August 20 into the Kommunion-kappelle (Communion Chapel) facing the great main doors of the Church of Holy Cross? The sides of the draped grille were covered with lovely summer blossoms and on both sides stood the community, happy to witness the ceremony that would usher Sister M. Josepha into the ranks of the professed Sisters.

Suddenly, the great doors opened and behind the grille stood Bishop Francis X. Schwaebl, silhouetted against the magnificent baroque main altar, ready to accept in the name of the Church the vows of Sister M. Josepha. One wonders as Sister offered herself as victim to be fixed to the cross by the three nails of Obedience, Chastity and Poverty was there given her any brief glimpse of the future crucifixion on her Calvary three thousand miles away.

---

5. Crawford, p. 99. Or *Archives*, Queen of the Rosary Motherhouse, Amityville.

CHAPTER IV

"A sower went out to sow seed . . . and
some fell on good ground and yielded
fruit a hundredfold."
(Matt. 13:4-9)

With the profession of Sister M. Josepha in 1839
began the career of one who was to live a full religious life in a short span and to exhibit all the facets
of Dominicanism.

Holy Cross Convent had accepted Maria Teresa
as a choir nun. She had completed her preparation
as a teacher in January of 1838, several months prior
to her entrance into the Community. The following
testimony of Sister M. Josepha's ability speaks for
itself:

"Teresa Witzlhofer, daughter of Simon Witzlhofer
and Catherine Wilhelm Witzlhofer at Ratisbon, has
finished the course of instruction required of the

teachers of girls and has acquired such perfection in all the arts that she may preside in any school for girls.

With much pleasure and as great a degree of conscientiousness, I award her this certificate as teacher in the feminine arts and recommend her highly. I cannot refrain from mentioning that she has shown an extraordinary gift of imparting this knowledge to the young."
Ratisbon, January 8, 1838
Royal District Inspection of the Upper City
                                        Wernziere, Inspector[1]

Subjects covered by the above certificate included: Religion and Bible History, Language, Writing, Mathematics, General History, German History, Geography, Natural History, Psychology, Drawing and Music.

Sister Josepha entered whole-heartedly upon her teaching career. This writer viewed the room on the upper story of the present convent which is now converted into a community room which once echoed with the voices of children responding to their loved young teacher in the pure white habit. It is not hard to imagine the bond between teacher and pupil as Sister Josepha saw in her young charges loving replicas of the seven brothers and sisters left behind. Her reputation as a teacher grew and her musical talent found a satisfying outlet in the songs, religious

---

1. Crawford, Rt. Rev. Eugene J., *Daughters of Dominic on Long Island* (Benziger, 1937), p. 215.

and patriotic, she encouraged her class to sing.

Meanwhile, the religious life of the Community had steadily deteriorated. In the years prior to Mother Benedicta Bauer's election as Prioress in 1845, Holy Cross Convent had more or less succumbed to the perverted ideas of religious discipline growing out of the influence of the secular authority on religious affairs. Things had come to such a pass that:

> ". . . the rules of enclosure had become very relaxed. Seculars took their meals with the Sisters in the Convent refectory; silence was not observed. Each Sister provided for herself and spent her own money independently."[2]

Sister M. Josepha was among the sixteen choir Sisters and six lay Sisters that comprised the Community. How far Sister Josepha went along with the alien spirit that pervaded the cloister once renowned for its strict observance of the Rule is all but impossible to determine. When discipline breaks down in a Community and laxity becomes the order of the day, sincere religious are torn between adherence to the principles they have so fervently espoused and demands of Christian charity that forbids the passing of judgment on the conduct of others except by those upon whom that responsibility rests.

That Sister Josepha ardently desired to live the

---

2. Kohler, Sister Mary Hortense, O.P., *Life and Work of Mother Benedicta Bauer* (Bruce, 1937), p. 50.

Dominican cloistered life in all its pristine beauty cannot be denied. This can readily be proved by the fact that only two years after Mother Benedicta Bauer introduced in "sweat, blood and tears" the reform of Holy Cross Convent, she did not hesitate to choose Sister Josepha, only eight years professed, to be one of the pioneers in the first foundation of the Ratisbon Motherhouse. Does a reformer choose rebellious, lax religious to set up a "Filiale?" Hardly! One need only glance at the type of woman Mother Benedicta was to realize what calibre of woman she would select to carry on her cherished reform.

Let us briefly examine the nature of the reform and try to understand something of the trials endured both by the reformer and the reformed.

To study the history of any Community caught in the throes of reform is to look deeply into the heartbreak of many souls. Few Religious Orders have escaped this peculiar trial since human beings constitute its bone and sinew, and human nature is prone to weakness. To maintain the high ideals of the original founder over a long period of time without expecting the erosion of time to eat away at its vitals is expecting perpetual miracles. Reform, too, indicates growth, since reform is change (mind you, not change for change sake); refusal to change breeds stagnation and stagnation spells eventual total destruction.

In 1845, six years after Sister Josepha promised to live according to the rule and constitution of the Dominican Community of the Holy Cross, Mother Benedicta Bauer, newly elected Prioress, determined to restore that rule in all its primitive observance. The Eve of All Saints was the auspicious moment selected by this astute observer of human nature to appeal gently but firmly to the grace hidden deep in the hearts of her subjects. She lifted their gaze to the infinite reward reserved for those who serve God faithfully while not hesitating to outline the eternal misery of those who flouted God's law after solemnly professing to observe it. She pointed to the great army of white-clad followers of Dominic who had achieved their goal through perfect adherence to the very rule by which they had chosen to live.

Sister Josepha felt her heart touched to its depths with the sincerity ringing in the voice of her Superior and an upsurge of renewed determination to strive after perfect observance followed. She had suffered during the past six years of her religious life the petty but real persecution that any religious is heir to who strives to adhere to strict observance in an atmosphere of laxity.

Did the entire community of 22 Sisters willingly embrace the restoration to liturgical prayer and penitential living introduced by Mother Benedicta? To answer in the affirmative is to exhibit a naïve approach to human nature "more inclined to evil than to good." Apparently there were:

"a number of holy souls among that group of cloistered nuns, who with desire had prayed and longed for the return of the primitive spirit and the peace and happinesss which accompanies the strict observance of the rule of the great St. Dominic. Such as these must have found a woman with the spirit of reform, filled with the courage of her convictions and willing to sacrifice herself for the community. And verily high courage was required to substitute observance for infraction, conformity for inconformity and regularity for irregularity."[3]

That there were some among "that number" who accepted the reform reluctantly, clinging tenaciously to their comforts so gratifying to human nature can be gleaned from the lines:

". . . and still there are some who do not heed the admonitions until they are forced to it by severe penances."[4]

and this was said two years after the reform had been inaugurated.

In the diary of Mother Benedicta Bauer we also note the intense sufferings she endured in her effort at reform, sufferings surely not caused by the "number . . . who prayed and longed for the return of the primitive spirit." Mother Benedicta writes in her diary under the date of June 15, 1854:

". . . ah, the rule book; with this book I am well acquainted. I have taken so much trouble upon

---

3. *Loc. cit.*
4. *Ibid.*, p. 57.

myself on account of this book—shed so many tears—have had so many misunderstandings. . . ."[5]

The reform was complete when Reverend Doctor Franz Schiml, confessor of the Sisters for nine years, wrote an up-to-date translation of the rule of Blessed Humbert, fifth Master General of the Order, accompanied by a German translation of the same Master General's explanation of the rule. His Grace, the Right Reverend Valentin von Riedel, himself visited the Convent to distribute the rule books among the Sisters. Sister Josepha received this precious document and set about the serious and prayerful study of its contents, so that she might be completely cognizant of the spiritual bonds uniting her with her saintly predecessors back to him whom she loved to call "Father Dominic."

It was surely during these anxious times that the soul of Sister Josepha was being tried by fire to prepare her for the special work carved out for her from all eternity by the Master Craftsman of the Church. Soon the cradle of Holy Cross, where her spiritual life had been nurtured, was to send her forth to carry the well-learned message to distant shores.

---

5. *Ibid.*, p. 73.

CHAPTER V

"Increase and multiply"
(Genesis 2:24)

Before attempting to describe the real vocation for which Sister Josepha had been invited by God into the ancient cloister of Holy Cross, Regensburg, that is, the founding of the Dominican Order in America, it might come as a surprise to some to learn this was her *second*, not her *first* pioneering venture.

As has already been mentioned in a previous chapter, Holy Cross Convent was the only Dominican Convent left standing when the ravages of secularization had done its worst. It was no accident nor mere chance that placed a woman of wide vision and dauntless courage at the helm in Holy Cross at this period in history.

Mother Benedicta, a true daughter of Dominic, looked out over the walls of Holy Cross to the beckoning Bavarian countryside and caught the echo of the

Dominican chant rising up from citadels of prayer set up by her and those to succeed her.

Her first dream was to acquire the suspended Augustinian Convent of St. Mary's, Niederviehbach. It had been designated a central convent for dispersed nuns after the secularization of 1803 and in 1846 Mother Benedicta received a favorable reply to her request of King Louis I of Bavaria to establish a branch house of Dominican Sisters there.

In the fall of 1847 the institution, now ranked as one of the outstanding educational establishments for girls in Germany, was solemnly opened. Sister M. Josepha was one of the four choir nuns to journey with two lay Sisters and Mother Benedicta to Niederviehbach. The trials and hardships of this first pioneering project was Sister Josepha's apprenticeship for the greater trials and hardships awaiting her in a few years.

Sister Amanda von Schenk, Superior until 1854 at Niederviehbach, describes these early years in a letter dated February 27, 1873:

> "Now it is twenty-five and a half years since Mother Benedicta founded Niederviehbach and brought us here from Ratisbon. Our way was not strewn with roses. We received many thorns, for to carry the cross after the Lord was often hard."[1]

---

1. Kohler, Sister Mary Hortense, O.P., *Life and Work of Mother Benedicta Bauer* (Bruce, 1937), p. 82.

At least in Niederviehbach, a former Monastery, all the familiar surroundings of monastic living were present. How utterly different was to be the setting for her second monastery. Added to separation from her beloved Holy Cross would be exile from her dear fatherland.

Sister Josepha was busily engaged in her teaching profession coupled with the living out of the monastic rules of a Dominican cloistered nun. Meanwhile, the busy Hands of Divine Providence were fashioning a new project deeply involving the unsuspecting, unassuming religious.

Early in 1851, a former resident of Ratisbon, Rev. Boniface Wimmer, a Benedictine from Latrobe, Pennsylvania, visited a relative at Holy Cross, a Sister Elizabeth Kissel. Father Wimmer was a missionary to the fingertips and during his visit spoke in glowing terms of the exciting apostolate in America. He drew graphic word-pictures of the crying need of the German immigrant for religious education for his offspring. How well he must have guessed the fire of zeal burning in the heart of Mother Benedicta as he saw mirrored in her eyes the rising flame from the spark he had ignited. America—a vast new world, was eagerly awaiting the tender hands of Dominic's daughters to harvest its overripe fields.

Mother Benedicta's zeal was catching. Sister Augustine Neuhierl was the first to seek permission to leave Ratisbon for America. The news of the visit and the proposed exodus reached St. Mary's during one of

Mother Benedicta's personal visits granted her at intervals by the Bishop who set aside the rules of enclosure.

Sister Josepha was nothing if she were not a real daughter of the missionary-minded Dominic. She also was fired by the recital of Mother Benedicta's recounting of Father Wimmer's story. Father Crawford caught the affinity between subject and Superior when he wrote:

> "Mother Benedicta's precepts were stored in the plastic and willing hearts of several young women who were destined to rise to positions of responsibility in the New World, and they in turn passed to their spiritual daughters the lessons of religious observance learned when they sat at the feet of their good Mother.
>
> These young Sisters were: (1) Sister Mary Josepha Witzlhofer. . . ."[2]

As Mother Benedicta recounted the stories so well told by the veteran missionary, Sister Josepha felt her pulse quicken and an urge rising in her soul that suffused her whole being. How gladly would she go to place her God-given talents at the disposal of the Giver, to spread His Kingdom in the receptive hearts of His children far from home. Sister Josepha confided her desire to be one of the little band of American

---

2. Crawford, Rt. Rev. Eugene J., *Daughters of Dominic on Long Island* (Benziger, 1937), p. 37.

missionaries and Mother Benedicta smiled her approval. It was two long years before her dream was realized.

We read in Sister Hortense:

". . . Father Wimmer promised that he, on his part would do all that he could do to make possible a new Dominican foundation. . . . But at this time it was impossible."[3]

Impossible! Why? It is difficult at this time to understand all the hidden springs that rose up to dam the flow. Looking into the account of the Dominicans' labors in America, "From Ratisbon's Cloisters" by Christine Sevier, we read:

"This generous zeal was, however, to be tried and tempered, to be put to the crucial test of delay. After prolonged consideration, Bishop Valentin Riedal, at that time ordinary of the diocese withheld the approbation and consent necessary for the inauguration of the hazardous venture from which conservative idealists would have recoiled, dismissing it instantly as prohibitive, aghast at the magnitude of the risks to be encountered."[4]

While Bishop Riedel was withholding permission, what was transpiring on both sides of the Atlantic?

---

3. Kohler, *op. cit.*, p. 92.
4. Sevier, *op. cit.*, p. 21.

Mother Benedicta's zeal, probably a much more powerful force in making the American foundation a reality than Abbot Wimmer's, was far from dampened by the Bishop's refusal. She wrote to Father Wimmer for details of the necessary steps to be taken to secure the success of the proposed venture when permission was granted. Several letters passed between her and Abbot Wimmer before she approached the Bishop again in 1853 for permission to open an American branch of Holy Cross. The letter to Bishop Riedel follows:

"Most Reverend Bishop
Gracious Lord:
    Two years ago the Most Reverend Father Boniface Wimmer, during his sojourn in Ratisbon called at the convent several times and repeatedly expressed his great desire of having Sisters of our convent come to the missions of America and there make a foundation of our Order, so that following the example of our Holy Father St. Dominic we might labor in the vineyard of the Lord, not only working out our own salvation, but also working for the salvation of so many neglected children. To accomplish this, Reverend Father Wimmer, repeatedly and very earnestly promised his cooperation, that he might, to use his own words, "make St. Dominic indebted to him."
    In January this year he wrote again explaining that since he returned to America he had given much attention to the project of founding a con-

vent of nuns of our Order. He consulted the Dominican Fathers whom he met at the Council of
Baltimore a year ago regarding the matter, and
Father Superior was quite pleased with his plans
for the immigration of German Dominican Sisters
and the making of a foundation in his territory in
which the temporal as well as the spiritual welfare
of the Sisters could be provided. The effect of this
offer was that the Sisters who had previously expressed their desire of immigrating now presented
their petitions anew and very earnestly begged
that they be permitted to accept Father Wimmer's
invitation. Hereupon the obedient undersigned informed Reverend Wimmer of their determination
and begged him to inform them what steps must
necessarily be taken in order to put their resolution
into effect.

His reply of April 14, was as follows: The
Sisters desirous of becoming missionaries should
journey immediately to St. Vincent's as their destination where they would remain for some time to
learn the English language under his direction and
*at the same time observe all religious obligations
of the Order undisturbed as religious.* The care of
all the rest would be assumed by Reverend Father
Wimmer as he definitely assured them in the letter
mentioned. In this letter he also says 'Ask your
Reverend Bishop for a Dimissory, that is, a Latin
testimonial to the effect that these Sisters (Each
Sister's name mentioned) are sent to the missions
in America to found a convent of their Order and

that *they are directed for the time being to me as their counselor and protector.'* In regard to the journey he informed us that he had given the Reverend Court Chaplain Mueller all necessary directions and we enclose the letter which Father Mueller has written in answer to ours.

The obedient undersigned humbly petition that your grace may give the aforementioned Dimissory for the two Choir nuns, Sister Josepha Witzlhofer and Sister Augustine Neuhierl and also for the lay Sisters Francesca Retter and Jacobina Riederer. Awaiting a gracious answer to this humble petition, we remain in profoundest reverence,

Your Grace's most humble and obedient,

M. Benedicta Bauer, Prioress

Antonina Malor, Subprioress"[5]

It is most interesting to note that while the above Dimissory was being sought in such good faith and childlike trust in the good missionary who first aroused their ardent hopes to be of service to the American missions, he, on his part, manifested a very vague grasp of the whole affair. He apparently was sincere in thinking they might first settle in Carrolltown, western Pennsylvania, but he made no definite plans. Too, he did receive a nebulous promise from the Dominican Fathers from Ohio that they would welcome Dominican Sisters into their midst; but here again no practical

---

5. *Holy Cross Chronicle,* Excerpt III, p. 8.

preparations were made for their actual arrival.

Possibly too, Dom Wimmer had, like all missionaries everywhere, enough to occupy fully several men and the added burden of responsibility for a new foundation with its subsequent taxing obligations began to appall him as he saw the vague dream suddenly becoming a reality. At any rate, he wrote to a friend on July 29, 1853:

> "In the near future I shall have to go to New York again to meet six (6) Dominican Sisters that the Convent of the Holy Cross of Ratisbon is sending me as a cross (as if I did not as yet have enough crosses). I am to look for a suitable place for them. Already letters for that purpose have been sent East and West. Perhaps I shall be able to locate them in Williamsburg, a suburb of New York City, where the German pastor and Vicar General Raffeiner is disposed to take them if the Archbishop permits it. Otherwise I must, for the time being, send my people out of the city to the farm and give the Sisters the house in Indiana, Pennsylvania, until such a time that I can find a suitable place for them."[6]

So, while Sister Josepha and her three companions prepared to transfer from one well-established religious house to settle at St. Vincent's "to observe all

---

6. Crawford, *op. cit.*, p. 42.

religious obligations of the Order undisturbed as religious," their "counselor and protector" was scanning the wide vistas of America for a place to settle them.

One is tempted at this point in the narrative to wonder what would have transpired had Sister Josepha the gift of clairvoyance. Could she have, ever so fleetingly, been given a glimpse of the Monastery cellar awaiting her, would the tree whose roots she was to plant have died aborning? I think not because her nature, although frail, housed a stalwart heart, steel tempered in the fires God lights to fashion heroic women.

CHAPTER VI

"Put out into the deep and lower your
nets for a catch"
(Luke 5:4)

The great adventure of Sister Josepha and her
companions was launched with the blessing of Bishop
von Riedcl who sent a favorable reply to Mother
Benedicta's request in a Dimissory:

"We, Valentin, by the Divine Mercy and the favor
of the Apostolic See, Bishop of Ratisbon.
    Since the Reverend Boniface of the Order of
St. Benedict, superior in North America, desires
that we send to America some Sisters from the
Holy Cross Monastery in Ratisbon well qualified
for educating young girls, we, therefore yielding
most gladly to his prayers having conferred in
council with the prioress and the conventuals of
said Monastery regarding the Sisters who expressed

their desire of going into the missions of America and having properly examined these Sisters, we send the following: The choir nuns, Maria Josepha Witzlhofer, and Maria Augustine Neuhierl, with the Sisters Maria Francesca Retter, and Maria Jacobina Riederer under the condition, however, that they remain in the congregation to which they are bound by their sacred vows and under the jurisdiction of the prioress of Holy Cross until such time as their numbers increase sufficiently to erect a new monastery in America, or in case of exigency that they be allowed to return to the Holy Cross Monastery. We, moreover, confirm the appointment of Maria Josepha Witzlhofer on whom the prioress has enjoined the government of the newly organized community. We, therefore, earnestly recommend these Sisters whose great zeal for promoting the honor of God we highly esteem, to the most Reverend and illustrious Ordinary of that diocese under whose jurisdiction they will be, requesting that he will receive them as daughters with all paternal affection and apostolic charity.

Given at Ratisbon, the Kingdom of Bavaria, May 29, 1853.

+ Valentin, Bishop of Ratisbon
Paintner, Secretary[1]

There are several interesting and important points in the above document which deserve a closer scrut-

---

1. *Holy Cross Chronicle,* Excerpt III, p. 2.

iny. The Bishop "properly examined the Sisters" and expressed his own high esteem for their great zeal for promoting the honor of God.

There are in every culture the cynics who by innuendoes raise doubts as to the motives spurring on noble souls. So there were, and perhaps there are still, the few who may as Msgr. Crawford puts it so well, attribute "escape into more verdant pastures for disappointed subjects"[2] as the moving force behind Sister Josepha's coming to America. The Bishop's high recommendation should put that ghost to rest forever.

Further, it should be remembered for future chapters, when the question of the legality of other foundations is raised, that the document does seem to embrace the entire Episcopate of the American Church as protectors of the Sisters. No specific Ordinary is named; the letter merely states "the most Reverend and illustrious Ordinary of that diocese under whose jurisdiction they will be."

Finally, the clause, "that they remain in the congregation to which they are bound . . . until such time as their numbers increase sufficiently to erect a new monastery in America," clearly granted the right to the properly-designated Superior to accept candidates; for, how else do numbers increase?

Here, at last, after two long years of patient waiting, the green light appeared and final preparations were begun by the Sisters. In the subdued hustle of

2. Crawford, Rt. Rev. Eugene J., *Daughters of Dominic on Long Island* (Benziger, 1937), p. 39.

gathering the necessary wardrobe (one might specu-
late endlessly on what it consisted of), Sister Josepha's
heart was a caldron of mixed emotions. She experienced moments of fear at the realization of the burden
Mother Benedicta had placed on her young shoulders,
she was just thirty-six years of age, in choosing her as
Superior of the small band. This in turn was replaced
by confident joy in the knowledge that innocent souls
were to be won for the Master she loved so tenderly.

Mother Benedicta gave the Sisters 4,000 gulden
($1,500) together with twenty chests of furnishings
for the Church and the Sisters' house amounting to
2,255 gulden. The Ludwig-Mission Verein supplied
the passage money. More precious than any material
gift was a "relic of the True Cross" given them by
Bishop Riedel whose fatherly interest in the Sisters
prompted him to pay a personal visit to them before
their departure.

Reverend Joseph Ferdinand Mueller, Court Chaplain of King Louis and business manager of the Ludwig-Mission Verein, assisted the Sisters in contacting
the various agencies for their journey and accompanied
them as far as Leipsig on their railway trip to the
port of Bremerhaven. Before leaving the small group,
his priestly concern prompted him to write a note of
introduction to the pastor of Most Holy Redeemer
Church asking his kindly assistance should the Sisters
be delayed in New York on their way to western
Pennsylvania. Mother Josepha little realized the value
of the missive as she gratefully tucked it away for

"possible" future use. It was to prove the "open sesame" to the mission fields of America!

Sister Josepha suffered greatly from the long train ride out of Bavaria. Physically spent and emotionally drained by the events of the past forty-eight hours, she ascended the gangplank of the "Germania" to begin the long, tiresome ocean crossing. She felt strange, bereft for the first time of her lovely Dominican habit, and a wave of utter loneliness wrapt her around like a heavy fog through which no penetrating ray of light shed comfort.

Ocean vessels in 1853 were a far cry from the luxurious floating palaces of 1970 and the Sisters as befitting their poverty did not travel first class. One's imagination need not be too vivid to appreciate even remotely what that twenty-five days must have exacted from all of them, particularly the gentle Superior. If the train ride had, in the words of Father Mueller, taken such a toll: "we were hardly one hour from Regensburg when good Josepha became deathly pale and soon began to vomit. . . . Poor Josepha had to go without breakfast and we were fearful for her,"[3] what must have been the physical distress of Sister Josepha through those seeming endless days and nights.

Finally, August 26 dawned cool, and the first glimpse of the sprawling country henceforth to be "home" was a welcome sight to the weary travelers. Along with the two hundred fourteen other passengers,

---

3. *Chronicle,* Letter of Father Mueller, July, 1853.

the Sisters gathered their belongings as the steamship prepared to dock at the foot of Franklin Street, a mile or so above the Battery. At eight o'clock Sister Josepha with her small community set foot on American soil and peered a bit anxiously into the sea of faces crowding the dock. Where was the friend whose letters had stretched a welcoming hand across the vast ocean to draw them here? Everyone seemed bent on his own affairs and no one took any notice of the four forlorn figures remaining on the dock as the crowds began to dwindle.

A rising fear threatened to stifle the breath of Sister Josepha as she began to realize their plight. Here they were, unrecognized as nuns in their strange secular clothing, totally unfamiliar with the language and at a loss what to do. But, Sister Josepha was far from an hysterical female! Her good common sense reminded her of the letter of introduction slipped so casually into her bag at Leipsig. She ignored the rising panic within and looked about for someone who might recognize the address on the envelope.

A kindly stevedore, taken by the air of modesty and other-worldliness of the four women who registered perplexity in their faces, turned to Sister Josepha. In some manner she was able to communicate her dilemma and a conveyance was secured to take them to the address on the letter "Church of the Most Holy Redeemer" about two miles distant from the pier.

And Father Wimmer? Where was he on the morning of August 26, 1853? To all appearances he had forgotten the whole affair. But appearances can be deceiving and one can scarcely believe that a man of his misionary zeal had dismissed the proposed project after such serious effort to locate the Sisters as is evidenced in his letter previously mentioned. According to historical records he had requested a friend, Father Balleis, a busy Newark pastor, to meet the Sisters since he was unexpectedly impeded. That Father Balleis did not appear is quite evident and perhaps we shall never ascertain the real reason for the failure.

"God writes with crooked lines," and surely the zigzag method used in bringing the first German Dominicans to Williamsburg can only evoke our deepest faith. For the Sisters arrived at the Redemptorist Rectory, were welcomed by the good Father Kleineidam and a lay Brother, and placed temporarily in the homes of trustworthy families in New York and Newark. Why Newark? Perhaps Father Balleis, arriving in the afternoon, too late for the "Germania's" docking, had been directed to the Redemptorist Church to find the nuns he had come to meet. Very likely he offered to take the two Sisters back with him until the blundering mess was cleared up.

Sister Josepha spent the next few days in fervent prayer, petitioning her Father to reveal His Will to His stranded daughters. His Will had determined from all eternity that the roots of Dominican Spirituality would sink deep in the furrowed soil of the German mission of Williamsburg. So, He sent His emissary, the

Very Reverend Stephen Raffeiner, pastor of the Church of the Most Holy Trinity and Vicar General of the Archdiocese of New York, to the Redemptorist Church on a visit, possibly to go to confession. There he learned that the Sisters from Ratisbon, mentioned to him a month before by Abbot Wimmer, had arrived. They were his for the asking, and he asked. Here, indeed, was the Will of God.

Did Sister Josepha question the change of plan? Did she wonder why Williamsburg and not Carrolltown, Pennsylvania, the original goal of the apostolic venture? Perhaps, but only momentarily, because true missionary that she was, Sister realized that children anywhere who needed her ministrations were her destined field of endeavor. Therefore, following the dauntless spirit of their Superior, the Sisters again put on their religious habits, bade a grateful farewell to their kind benefactors and crossed the East River; and so it was in God's own time, in God's own way that Brooklyn received Dominic's torch bearers.

CHAPTER VII

"With men this is impossible but with
God all things are possible."
(Matt. 19:26)

Before landing with Sister Josepha and her three
companions in Williamsburg on September 2, 1853,
it is important for an understanding of their future
labors to examine the environment into which they
came.

Williamsburg was at that period of her history a
center of German-American life. As Napoleon swept
across Europe in the early 19th Century, many German immigrants found escape in the New World. New
York was a natural stopping-off place with its well-
developed harbor, and the fertile soil across ths East
River lured many a German farmer into the area of
Williamsburg. Here the customs and language of the
Fatherland were continued.

By 1840, the religious needs of these German Catholics, mostly truck farmers, prompted the zealous pastor of St. Nicholas, Father Raffeiner, to resign and go over to Bushwick, the edge of Williamsburg, where he generously purchased land with his own money. On October 10, 1841, the cornerstone of the first Holy Trinity Church was laid. At the time of the Sisters' arrival the second Church of the Holy Trinity parish was in the process of erection.

The country itself was seething with unrest, an unrest to erupt into Civil War within seven years. Bigotry was rampant. On the very evening the Sisters left the "Germania," the infamous American Party was spewing its vitriolic poison against the Papacy and all its works into the willing ears of fellow bigots in New York. Laws were urged denying the right of property ownership to anyone submitting to a foreign bishop. Both they and the Know-Nothing Party were to be a source of concern to Sister Josepha and the infant community.

As Sister Josepha approached the Church building, she looked about expectantly for the Monastery where, at long last, she and her dear companions might find again the regular religious life so sorely missed during the hectic days of the past month. Father Raffeiner had not mentioned the convent in his brief description of the apostolic work awaiting them in his parish. It is all but impossible to bring full appreciation to the polarity between the well-structured, quiet seclusion of a cloistered community life and the non-structured, molelike existence into which Sister Josepha was introduced that Friday.

Their Monastery was a basement (another word for cellar) consisting of three rooms—kitchen, community room and dormitory under the rectory. Enclosure was to consist of a locked door leading to the above apartments. A letter of Dom Wimmer, who incidently arrived on the scene a week late, gives an eloquent description of the living conditions of the Sisters:

"Because no convent is there, we were obliged to lodge the Sisters in the rectory which adjoins the old church. Do not be alarmed at this. The pastor, the above-named Vicar General, is an old Father, a holy priest, and has only one curate. The rectory is spacious. I remained four days with him to arrange everything. The four Sisters already after the first week have a complete enclosure as regards the outside—the people; and also interiorly with regard to the priests. Naturally they are in considerably close quarters, but it is satisfactory. . . . At the same time I bought four iron, very comfortable bedsteads, so that I might see whether there was sufficient room; we found that there was additional space for a table and a chest or bureau. The pastor who lives on the upper floor has access only to the kitchen. I arranged to make even this part of the enclosure by locking the door to his quarters. I had a partition made near the outside door so that now they receive there only mail and no one has access to their house.

Thus I succeeded in making an uninterrupted

or strictly private passageway which leads to the church and also to a large room under the church where the Sisters may store away their clothes, or if they wish, they may use it for sleeping quarters. . . . The School also adjoins the church."[1]

As Sister Josepha viewed the scene described above, her thoughts flew back to the hallowed walls of Holy Cross nestled in the Bavarian hills near the beautiful Danube. Here, in their cellar, she was to erect a new Holy Cross, a tree nurtured, as it were, in the dark, damp underground of Holy Trinity— roots sunk so deep that its branches would literally reach out to cover the four corners of this sprawling land. From the Pacific to the Atlantic, Holy Cross in America would send her daughters to bring the "good news" to thousands of America's youth from kindergarten to university level.

However, none of this comforting future lightened the weight of dismay and foreboding that gripped the heart of the young superior. She was, however, a true daughter of Dominic, who quickly adjusted to situations and with an encouraging smile for her subjects Sister Josepha stepped across the threshold of her "new monastery."

That she quickly adjusted is evident in the fact that a few days after this jolting experience Sister Josepha

---

1. Crawford, Rt. Rev. Eugene J., *Daughters of Dominic on Long Island* (Benziger, 1937), p. 42, 54.

and Sister Augustine stood ready to welcome the 140 young students who came to get their first glimpse of the white-clad Sisters who had crossed the ocean to instruct them. What courage these two women showed! Viewed from the vantage point of one-hundred-and-sixteen years, accustomed as we have grown to the latest pedagogical techniques and equipment, we can only marvel at the stamina of our two Dominican forebears who succeeded in the face of such obstacles. For succeed they did! These Sisters, as Father Crawford reminds us, "were not awkward tyros, but highly trained and accomplished women, supplying a type of teaching far superior to that which the tow-headed and rosy-cheeked youngsters had been accustomed."[2]

So deeply impressed were the parents at the high calibre of the instruction their children received, that word quickly spread throughout the area and the enrollment leaped. Even Abbot Wimmer was impressed. He wrote to the Abbot of Metten, Gregory Scherr, on Christmas Eve, 1853:

"God seems to bless this undertaking abundantly. Before the arrival of the Sisters, two men teachers never had more than 150-170 boys and girls together and now the Sisters alone have 225 girls in their classes and are expecting more from the godless public school."[3]

---

2. *Op. cit.*, p. 64
3. *Op. cit.*, p. 65.

Two hundred and twenty-five girls and expecting more! And this within three months of their arrival. Imagine that number, divided between two teachers, not in one grade but in several grades—and one might well be appalled in this twentieth century when a teacher finds one grade of forty youngsters a burden that taxes her physical and mental capacity to the hilt.

Coupled with the strain of fulfilling their teaching obligations under such adverse circumstances, was an even greater strain of endeavoring to live their full monastic life in their cramped quarters under the rectory. Here, they returned each day "to wrap themselves against the wind howling through the chinks in the wall; to try to sing the Office, to prepare the next day's work, and then to crawl shiveringly to bed."[4]

What heroism was demanded of what scripture calls "the weaker sex" during that first winter of 1853. Sister Josepha's motherly heart bled as she shared the sufferings of her sorely-tried children. Her sympathy and encouragement enfolded them like a protecting cloak during those early days of privation. She did everything within her power to lessen their hardships and uphold their strength. Like the valiant woman of the Gospel, her own courage held the little band together and tenaciously she trusted her heavenly Father who "feeds the birds of the air and clothes

---

4. Crawford, *op. cit.*, p. 67.

the lilies of the field." Affairs could not get worse; so, they had to get better.

Before relief came, however, the rigors of pioneering had exacted a heavy toll. Already, Sister Francesca Retter's health had begun to fail and the unmistakable signs of tuberculosis were evident in her hacking cough and continual loss of weight. By the Spring of 1855, the first victim demanded as the price for the flowering of Dominican life in America succumbed. Sister Francesca died May 22, 1855.

Sister Josepha recognized the impossibility of continuing to function under the crushing burdens of their present living conditions. With her shrewd "common sense" she had spent $1,200 of the $1,600 brought from Ratisbon to purchase a lot on the corner of Graham and Montrose Avenues for the site of a future convent. With the rest of the money used for necessities for themselves and the school (they were evidently expected to maintain the latter), the financial status of the community was precarious in the extreme. A tuition fee of $.25 a week per pupil was their only income.

Her trust in Divine Providence bore fruit when the Shepherd for the Diocese, Most Reverend John Loughlin, D.D., newly-appointed Bishop of the newly-erected diocese of Brooklyn, offered her a loan of $4,000 for the purchase of a more suitable dwelling. Oh, the joy that must have flooded the soul of Sister Josepha as she set about preparing to release her dear Sisters from their damp imprisonment of the past few months.

Between their lot and the new church stood a small

house owned by a Mr. Gunther. It was purchased and the deed given to the Bishop. With the exuberance of children set free, the Sisters began to renovate their little convent. Very special attention was given to the furnishing of the best room as the Guest Room for Emmanuel—God with us. For so long they had been deprived of His dear Presence among them.

At last, on May 16, 1854, after nine months, as it were, in the womb of mother earth, Dominic's daughters emerged and took up their dwelling in the small convent. A year later, as previously noted, Sister Francesca died.

This chapter of the early struggles of Sister Josepha and her pioneer group might be fittingly closed with Msgr. Crawford's comment on their first loss:

"Truly the first Sisters were crucified and most aptly then was a crucifix placed in the dead hand of this first victim of the hardships of pioneer life. On October 19, 1896, forty-one years after the death of Sister Francesca, her remains, together with those of Mother Josepha and other Sisters who had been interred in Holy Trinity Cemetery were exhumed and re-buried in the Novitiate Cemetery at Amityville. Of Sister Francesca's wasted body there remained a few bones and the whole left hand, brown and mumified, still grasping the crucifix"[5]

_____

5. *Op. cit.*, p. 71.

CHAPTER VIII

"One sows, another reaps! I have sent
you to reap that on which you have not
labored. Others have labored, and you
have entered into their labor."
(John 4:35)

A brighter day was dawning; the sacrifices of the
past year, accepted patiently, had merited God's loving benediction on His tried servants. Like the Israe-
lites of old, exiled in a foreign land, far from the
familiar haunts of happier days, the sight of the
Promised Land brought unutterable joy to their weary
hearts. So, Sister Josepha saw in the acquisition of
their little convent a haven of prayer and regular
observance; a promise of rich harvests to be gleaned
in joy by hands other than those who had cast the
seed in tears.

During the trying months that had passed, Sister
Josepha had written several times to Mother Bene-
dicta (none of which letters are extant) begging for
Sisters to help relieve the almost unsupportable burden

of teaching more than 200 children. Her letters bore fruit. Mother Benedicta, beset as she was by depletion of numbers because of several foundations in Germany, nevertheless, heeded the cry from her faithful daughter.

Three choir Sisters responded to the call for volunteers from Mother Benedicta and on May 9, 1855, Sister Michaela Braun, Sister Seraphine Staimer, and Sister Emilia Barth arrived at the Williamsburg convent to swell the ranks of the pioneers to seven. All three recruits were teachers. The group was seven for only ten days for the death on the 19th reduced the number to six.

What memories of the dear Bavarian Monastery did the three new arrivals revive in the minds of the toil-worn original missionaries, memories long tucked away as luxuries not to be indulged for fear they might weaken the resolve of these stalwart women to do the Master's work. How hungry they were and how avidly they consumed all news of the dear companions at Holy Cross. The three fresh recruits acted like a blood transfusion on the over-worked Sisters and new vigor coursed through them as they set about planning for the years ahead. Little did any of them realize the tremendous role each of these women (Sister Michaela returned to Ratisbon after two years in Williamsburg) would play in the expansion and development of the Community. Both would in turn be Prioress of the Brooklyn Community.

Sister Josepha buoyed by the response to her appeal for help and conscious of the need to provide proper living conditions for her growing community, began to envision a real convent. This, she planned, would be complete with a chapel, community room, refectory and an adequate number of sleeping rooms. To build meant money and that was a rare commodity among the Sisters. Sister Seraphine had brought with her a gift of 6,000 florins from the Ludwig-Mission Verein with a promise of 1,6000 annually for six years. This gift was the result of an appeal by Father Mueller, the Court Chaplain, who had already indebted the Sisters to him in 1853.

Sister Josepha was always humbly grateful for any assistance and in one of her letters (only two are extant) she thanked King Ludwig I:

"Letter of the Superior, Mother Josepha Witzlhofer in the name of her fellow-Sisters in Williamsburg; May 17, 1855 to King Ludwig of Bavaria:
. . . Your Majesty has deigned to send us, who came here from Ratisbon two years ago, a generous gift for the building of an educational institution. This enables us with the help of God soon to lay the cornerstone of the much desired building where we can in future live according to religious discipline and order, where the Divine Praises will rise to God at appointed times and the poor abandoned children may be instructed in their religion and drawn to God."[1]

---

1. Crawford, Rt. Rev. Eugene J., *Daughters of Dominic on Long Island* (Benziger, 1937), p. 73.

From their meager income, the Sisters began to put aside whatever they could spare toward the proposed project. In two years they had saved about $2,000. Confidence in God was characteristic of Sister Josepha. The lot on the corner of Graham and Montrose Avenues already was theirs through her wise purchase and foresight that first year. Here, work was begun on the new convent on the feast of St. John the Baptist, June 24, 1857. One must have lived in cramped quarters and watched a spacious convent being erected to understand the thrill of expectancy experienced by the Sisters as they saw their future Monastery rising.

By November all was ready. Bishop Loughlin dedicated the building on November 9, 1857, the feast of All the Saints of the Dominican Order, and named it the Convent of the Holy Cross. Ratisbon had its replica in America.

A very important footnote in "Daughters of Dominic on Long Island," page 76, throws light on the status of the community at this time:

"Although both the Williamsburg and Ratisbon convents disputed until about 1863 or 1864 concerning the actual time of the incardination of the Williamsburg Community as a Brooklyn Diocesan Community and although there is a regrettable absence of documents confirming the change of canonical status, November 9, 1857 may be considered the birthday of the Brooklyn Dominicans, and the granting of full authority to Mother Josepha as Mother Prioress."[2]

According to the above, Holy Cross, Brooklyn, became "de jure" an independent convent and Mother Josepha an independent Prioress. This follows from the fact that the very erection of the convent fulfilled the condition laid down by Bishop Riedel for independence of the community from the jurisdiction of the Prioress of Holy Cross, Ratisbon. Those conditions may be recalled in the letter of Dimissory quoted elsewhere, "under the condition that they remain in the Congregation to which they are bound . . . until such time as their numbers increase sufficiently to erect a new Monastery in America."

It is quite obvious that the one to determine that "time" should be the one under whose jurisdiction the Sisters were living, that is, Bishop Loughlin, Bishop of Brooklyn. That he approved the erection of and blessed the Monastery is proof sufficient that he considered the separation "de jure" and Mother Josepha as the independent Prioress.

Was Mother Josepha aware of the canonical implication inherent in the erection of the new convent? Did Bishop Loughlin sit down and step by step unfold the complicated structure thrown up by canon law to protect religious communities, particularly contem-

---

2. *Op. cit.*, p. 64.

plative communities? It is preposterous to think so!

Bishop John Loughlin was a missionary Bishop only recently consecrated to the newly-erected diocese of Brooklyn embracing all of Long Island. Rome granted extensive powers to men under such circumstances and the Propagation, under whose jurisdiction he operated, "grants to its missionary bishops the widest faculties and allows them vast discretionary powers to cope with situations wherein it is difficult to have recourse to Rome because of insufficient facilities of communication."[3]

Meanwhile, the joy of the Sisters knew no bounds as they settled into regular routine and enclosure. Mother Josepha, totally oblivious of the heavy cross of misunderstanding being fashioned for her decided that since they now had the accommodations, she must again appeal to her dear Mother Benedicta for additional Sisters to ease the workload of the Sisters:

"We have four hundred children taught in only three divisions; send us, therefore, more Sisters."[4]

At the time of her request, Mother Josepha was unaware of the storm raging around her beloved Prioress. Human nature does not radically change with the assumption of a religious habit. Christ, Him-

---

3. Crawford, Rt. Rev. Eugene J., *Daughters of Dominic on Long Island* (Benziger, 1937), p. 81.
4. *Archives,* Holy Cross Convent, Ratisbon.

self, had His Judas, and religious communities have throughout history suffered by harboring in their bosom persons, religious in name only, who become purifying agents for the rest of the members. Holy Cross, Ratisbon, was no exception.

Two religious, let them be nameless, created chaos in the community by their attitude and after being penanced, appealed to the new bishop, Bishop Ignatius von Synestry. In a later chapter, more will be said of the above-named Bishop. In the present situation, it is obvious that he was hasty in judgment and biased by acquainting himself with only one side of the controversy. He demanded the resignation of Mother Benedicta on the testimony of the two dissidents which order Mother complied with on June 10, 1858. Mother Mary Agnes Rosenloehner succeeded her.

To the cross-laden ex-Prioress, the letter of appeal from Mother Josepha must have seemed like a Simon of Cyrene lifting the other end of the crushing cross. She had the true spirit of a missionary and had years before, in fact, as far back as the first talk about the American missions by Father Wimmer, longed to go to distant shores to spread God's Kingdom. Now, at last, she was free to satisfy her desire. Christine Sevier writes of this occasion:

"The reader will have recognized in Mother Benedicta that religious of large sympathies and quiet impulses who as Prioress of Ratisbon had first conceived the project of sending the Dominican Sisters of the jurisdiction to America. It is now appointed that she should join them, see with her own eyes the work her generous spirit had created, share herself the hardships her daughters were enduring and for which she was so largely responsible — to practically demonstrate the sincerity of her enthusiasm when it became possible for her actually to become associated with the propaganda.[5]

By September of 1858 everything was in readiness for the last of the recruits from Ratisbon to set out for the Williamsburg Holy Cross. Mother Benedicta took with her, Sister Thomasina Ginker, Sister Cunigunda Schell and a candidate, Crescentia Traubinger. They arrived at the newly-erected convent on October 29, 1858.

The natural question arising at this point is, did Mother Benedicta intend to found an independent Motherhouse or did she intend to join the Sisters who had come to America earlier to add to their strength? From the Holy Cross Chronicle it is clear that the object was to found an independent Motherhouse:

"... The object of the journey was first, to remain at Williamsburg for some time where in the newly-founded convent the language and the customs of the country might be acquired, and secondly, to

---

5. Sevier, Christine, *From Ratisbon Cloister*, p. 38.

establish a new congregation with her companions when the opportunity would offer itself."[6]

With the arrival of Mother Benedicta and her three companions, the number of Sisters swelled to ten. Up to that date, no American candidates had been received by Holy Cross, Brooklyn.

What a contrast the living conditions of the American Dominicans must have presented to the Mother Prioress whose whole tenure had been spent restoring the primitive rule with all its restrictions to the Convent at Ratisbon. She, in her later years as pioneer foundress in the mid-west, must have come to appreciate the mitigations and dispensations that pioneer living makes imperative. Also, as a true Dominican she well knew the built-in flexibility which the wise Dominic had incorporated in his constitutions. The reaction of the newcomers is best seen through the eyes of one of them, Sister Thomasina, who wrote to her parents soon after her arrival:

"I am enchanted with the beautiful little convent and the friendly reception of our dear Sisters. America would have an attraction for me even as a secular, but in the convent I have the same order and work as in Germany. I was not lonesome for a moment. I have the boys' school, and there are

6. *Chronicle*, Holy Cross Convent, Ratisbon, Excerpt V., p. 2.

very dear children among the group. They are docile and good. The school is under the Church — simply boarded off. There is a great scarcity of priests. Although there is much work, there is plenty of nourishment. . . . Do not worry about me, because I am well taken care of. All the dear Sisters received me with the most sincere love.— In our beautiful chapel Christ is enthroned in the Holy Sacrament."[7]

Here we have a glimpse of the daily life of the little convent of Holy Cross. Mother Josepha welcomed her dear Mother Benedicta and companions with wide-open arms. For the next twenty months the increase in their ranks made admission of more students feasible. Mother Benedicta, while awaiting a favorable opportunity to move farther west and establish an independent Motherhouse, used her musical talents to enhance the education of the students.

At long last, the small community began to attract young women to their ranks. As applicants came, Mother Benedicta felt the shortage of teachers was eased and she took steps to carry out her plan to leave Williamsburg. With her went Sister Thomasina, her faithful companion. Sister Cunigunda Schell and Crescentia Traubinger chose to remain. Mother Josepha refunded the expenses born by Mother Benedicta

---

7. Kohler, Sister Mary Hortense, O.P., *Life and Work of Mother Benedicta Bauer* (Bruce, 1937), p. 156, 7.

for the passage of the two who stayed at Williamsburg. With this, she also gave Mother Benedicta 750 guldens which remained of Sister Jacobina's dowry, a gesture prompted by the caustic letter from Ratisbon on May 12, 1860. Subsequent chapters will quote at length from this letter as we examine the circumstances that caused it.

CHAPTER IX

"And he who does not take up his cross
and follow me, is not worthy of me."
(Matt. 10:38, 39)

At this point in history, removed by a hundred-
year span, one might find it difficult to understand the
serious turn of events affecting deeply the life of the
Foundress of the Dominican Sisters of Holy Cross.
The Master, the first cross bearer, rarely permits the
sign of His ignominy to be absent from any earthly
undertaking destined for success. Suffering is the
normal price paid by anyone with the temerity to ex-
pand His kingdom. Mother Josepha was to pay that
price in full. Misunderstanding was to dog her steps
for the next few years, a misunderstanding made all
the more poignant for one whose motives were above
reproach.

To bring some awareness to the problems, it will be
necessary to retrace our steps a bit to sift some of the
accumulated data in an effort to uncover the truth.

First, there was the physical problem of distance from the Motherhouse with the subsequent elapse of many months between questions asked by Mother Josepha and answers received from Ratisbon. No cable crossed the Atlantic in the year 1855.

Secondly, with the coming of Mother Benedicta and her companions in 1858, the interest in the American foundation seemed to have come to an end. Ratisbon's concern about her "Filiale" all but disappeared.

Then there was the erection and blessing of the Holy Cross Convent by Bishop Loughlin in 1857 which event automatically made Mother Josepha Prioress with freedom to act independently. This was referred to briefly in the previous chapter and will be dealt with at greater length in the following pages.

When Sister Josepha arrived in New York on that Friday morning in 1853 and by default came to Brooklyn instead of the supposed journey's end, Carrolltown, Pennsylvania, there was an interested party who expressed disappointment that he had not known of the Sisters' plight. That person was Reverend Ambrose Buchmeier, Capuchin pastor of St. Nicholas Church in Second Street, New York. He upbraided his friend, Dom Wimmer, for failing to inform him of the arrival of the Sisters.

During the subsequent difficult years of striving to remain afloat in the midst of such violent adverse winds, the Superior and her group were befriended by Father Buchmeier who acted as their extraordinary confessor. Therefore, when the good priest asked

Mother Josepha for some Sisters to staff his girls' school in February 1858 with a promise of a small convent ready for their residence, the grateful Superior was inclined to grant his request. However, a year and a half was to elapse before the proposal became an actual fact.

Even to suppose that Mother Josepha would consider acting completely on her own in such an important venture, is to label her ignorant, incompetent and proud, characteristics alien to her character and certainly absent in any of her past actions no matter how biasly scrutinized. She certainly was aware of the threat of excommunication hurled against those religious who dared to erect a new convent "without the consent of the General Chapter and of the Bishop of that diocese in which the convent was to be founded."[1]

Just what procedure did Mother Josepha follow? From what we have ascertained from a study of her method of action to date, we might be sure she proceeded prudently in the matter. She did not precipitously plunge into the venture as can be seen in the lapse of time (one and a half years) between the request and the decision. Normal procedure would have been to request permission first, from the Motherhouse in Ratisbon of which Mother Josepha still considered Holy Cross, Brooklyn, a "Filiale"; then, from Archbishop Hughes of New York into whose jurisdic-

---

1. *Constitutions of the Sisters of Ratisbon,* Edition of 1873, Chapter XXXII, p. 102.

tion the Sisters were to come; finally, from Bishop Loughlin out of whose diocese the Dominicans would go.

According to Msgr. Crawford who spent a great deal of time searching through archives and documents, there is no trace anywhere that Mother Josepha asked anyone. Yet — "Mother Josepha would not have dared to act on her own. The obvious conclusion is that she acted on the advice and authority of Bishop Loughlin."[2]

After mature deliberation, Mother Josepha, who heeded the words of her Founder, St. Dominic, "The seed will fructify if it is sown; it will but molder if horded," finally broke up her little group and sent Sister M. Augustine, who had borne with her the trials and tribulations of the early pioneering, as Superior, accompanied by Sister M. Cunegund, teacher, and Sister M. Rosa, a lay Sister. The die was cast and the storm to break upon her was not long in coming.

The reader will recall that Mother Benedicta was living at Williamsburg during this period waiting patiently for an opportunity to strike out into the wilderness and establish another community. She had at last received a favorable answer from the Provincial of the Dominican Fathers of Somerset, Ohio, requesting her to come. It is probable that Mother Benedicta recognized only local authority in Mother Josepha since we find her requesting permission from Mother

---

2. Crawford, Rt. Rev. Eugene J., *Daughters of Dominic on Long Island* (Benziger, 1937), p. 81.

Agnes Rosenloehner, her successor, to accept the invitation proffered by the Dominican Fathers.

We shall quote the answer of Mother Agnes in full since it reveals the attitude of the Ratisbon authorities toward Mother Josepha's apparent insubordination:

Ratisbon, May, 12, 1860

"Dear Mother Benedicta:

Your circumstance I can understand in a measure, but it is impossible for me to help you. You declare that it would be an aid to you if you received my permission to go elsewhere. The following is the bishop's reply:

'Those in America must become independent. But before taking that step they must declare if it be their intention to stay in America or to return to the Motherhouse. They need not come immediately, but they must declare their intention.'

Perhaps the best thing for me would be to add no further remarks of my own because, after all I can only say, 'become independent and then do what you consider the best.' The Reverend Spiritual Director Schoettle told me there was a decision of the Holy Father to the effect that branch houses must become independent. Whether this applied to all convents I cannot say.

I have informed Sister Josepha that Williamsburg must comply with this order, and I have written to her several times to this effect. But the letters, it seems, do not reach their destination. The first one, however, was received. I am certain of that, for the Sisters acted as if they were insane and declared they would not agree to any separation from the Motherhouse. They even stated that they would all return to Europe. It is most singular — these people may found convents in America without our permission — may appoint subjects to these houses without asking us — and may leave them at will. Most singular dependence on the Motherhouse! I have already told Sister Josepha that she can no longer claim subjects or financial aid from the Motherhouse. What new tricks will these American Sisters be up to when they hear again that they must become independent?

In so far as you are concerned, you are the best judge of your own case. You do not want to come back to us, and no good will come of your staying with those Sisters. Your only request to us is permission to leave the convent. Oh my God, this permission, according to my opinion means so much! In the first place the Prioress of Holy Cross Convent cannot give you this permission. Secondly, it is equivalent to the Motherhouse opening a new foundation through you, and we should be under obligations to supply a sufficient number of subjects and be responsible for the support of the foundation. To undertake teaching together with Sister Thomasina will lead to no good results. My opinion is this:

If you know that a Dominican Nun would be allowed to work as a missionary and found a new house as you, or rather, Sister Thomasina writes, then certainly we would have no objections. Indeed, everyone of us would wish to be of service to you, so that you might obtain your goal. I wrote to Sister Josepha that she must pay back the one thousand francs belonging to Sister Jacobina, because my subjects are not willing to make a gift of that sum to Williamsburg. In case you find a little place of your own in America, then Sister Josepha is to turn over the thousand francs to you. The Sisters here want you to have it.

I wrote to Reverend Abbot Wimmer and pleaded with him to find a little place of your own for you. I gave the letter to a girl by the name of Wiemer. This girl wishes to enter the convent in Williamsburg — perhaps she is there already. I would so much like to help you, but every aid I would offer would be contrary to our Constitutions. I wish that help would come too but I myself cannot extend any, because the whole affair is contrary to my conscience and convictions.

You may do as you wish as long as I shall not be concerned in any transaction. Therefore, you people in America should become independent, and then you could adjust yourselves according to the regulations which exist in America. You could spread out and work in the missions as the Lord provides occasions. I cannot give a more definite decision than this, and it may probably grieve you.

Sister Thomasina will tell you the news I am
writing to her. God will surely help you as He has
always helped in the past. Let these be the words
of comfort.

From your

Mother Agnes[3]

The above letter speaks volumes and in the interest of truth and justice demands a close analysis. It
must be quite evident to the reader that Ratisbon, at
least those in authority in Ratisbon, were eager to rid
themselves of an obligation which had become an em-
barrassing burden on the Motherhouse. Mother Agnes
speaks several times of the letters sent to Mother Josepha demanding the American foundation become independent. What was the date of that first letter
requesting Mother Josepha to set up an independent
community? It could not have been before Mother
Benedicta's resignation. That would place it late in
1858. For Mother Josepha to recoil from separation
when the wounds inflicted during the pioneering days,
so vivid because so recent, were scarcely healed, is
quite understandable. To label such a reaction insanity is hardly fair. It was merely the natural reluc-
tance of a wise woman to expose her still infant
community to the threat of possible extinction because
of limited funds and few members. Prudence is scarcely insanity.

Mother Agnes further speaks in seething tones of

---

3. *Archives,* Sisters of St. Dominic, Racine, Wisconsin.

the independent action of Mother Josepha in "found-ing convents (note the plural) in America without our permission — may appoint subjects to these *houses* without asking us — and may leave them at will."

One Convent, Second Street, had been founded, not several, and there is no record that any Sister had left it. Was the information coming to the Motherhouse exaggerated in the reading? Was it misinterpreted? Was it hearsay? Or, in charity, may one ascribe the causticity of the remarks, "Most singular dependence on the Motherhouse!" and "What new tricks will these American Sisters be up to when they hear again that they must become independent," to a total ignorance of the circumstances of the American mission and a reflection of the unrest in the house at Ratisbon which took its toll of Mother Agnes?

Be that as it may, the letter certainly brought great pain to the sensitive heart of Mother Josepha. Her whole religious life had been marked by loyalty to authority. Surely, Mother Benedicta herself could be the witness to that fact. Yet, Mother Benedicta was no comfort during this trial since she, too, was suffering from the decision of two of her companions, Sister Cunigunda and the postulant Crescentia Traubinger, to remain in Williamsburg. This resulted "in a cool-ness" in the relationship between the two women.

The clouds gathering around Mother Josepha gave no sign of lifting. Rather, the gloom deepened as ominous news reached the Williamsburg group that Mother Agnes had taken steps to lay the whole matter of insubordination before episcopal authority.

4

Bishop Valentin von Riedel, the fatherly Bishop who had blessed their first venture, was succeeded by Bishop Ignatius von Synestry. It was he who demanded the resignation of Mother Benedicta after a onesided hearing of her columniators. He was totally unfamiliar with the American scene. It was to Bishop von Synestry that Mother Agnes presented an official summary of her policy. And on October 26, 1860, the Bishop sent the following official decree of himself and his Consultors to Mother Josepha:

"A convent in which there are only 3 professed Sisters and 4 novices is in all things in a condition of defect. Neither is it possible to observe the Holy Rule in all its entirety nor is it possible to make the convent self-subsisting. The affiliated Convent in Williamsburg has gone against the Spirit of the Order and the Rule of St. Dominic and even against the obedience it is obliged to render to the Motherhouse. You neglected to get in connection with the Motherhouse. It is possible for newly founded convents to become independent if it is done according to the Spirit of the Order and according to Rome, but you have through the foundings of new affiliations in New York and Somerset without the consent of the Motherhouse to whom you are subject blamably worked against your own independence.

Such conduct against the rule and obedience for which no authority, no privilege, from Rome can be shown, caused the high authority to inform

Rome and in the meantime all former acts by means of which new affiliations from the yet dependent affiliated Convent in Williamsburg could be founded are to be considered null and void."

(Signed) J. V. Regar, Vicar General[4]

Mother Josepha received the communication with a shock. She summoned her companions, Sister Seraphine and Sister Emilia to reveal the contents of the letter and to discuss its implications. It was quite apparent to all three, as they examined the decree, that there were serious discrepancies in it, possibly due to mis-information. Mother Benedicta had permission from Ratisbon, not from Mother Josepha, to set out for Ohio. Therefore, it was not a foundation stemming from Williamsburg. Further, the number of Sisters in the two convents, Holy Cross and Second Street, totalled five professed and four novices.

Mother Josepha immediately sought the advice of her own Ordinary, Bishop Loughlin, who reassured her as to her own personal position and the status of the two convents. Had he not canonically erected the Brooklyn Motherhouse in 1857 "de jure" creating an independent community and bestowing on Mother herself the right to act as he had advised?

Again, however, and unfortunately, there is nothing in writing to confirm the above conclusion. But, surely, if Rome had acted on the recommendation of Bishop von Synestry both the Brooklyn and New York Com-

4. *Archives*, Diocese of Ratisbon.

munities would have ceased to exist. Neither Bishop Loughlin nor Mother Josepha were censured either by the Propaganda or the Master General as Msgr. Crawford testifies after a thorough research through the Archives of the Casa Generalizia of the Dominican Order and the Brooklyn Diocesan Archives.

Bishop von Synestry was, as Father Schrems of Ratisbon puts it "somewhat radical; inclined to take extreme measures without sufficient examination of facts, over-hasty and one-sided. . . . One so inclined might easily issue a decree of nullity on totally insufficient grounds and without sufficiently examining the law of the facts."[5] He had in his letter of Dimissory to Mother Benedicta Bauer on August 15, 1858 called Mother Josepha "prioress of those Sisters who have already gone to the missions"[6] thus, at least inadvertently implying independent authority on her part.

Mother Josepha, reassured by the counsel of Bishop Loughlin, who recognized her right to act independently, continued to direct the Sisters and the school under her care. Although the actual date of separation remains undetermined, it would seem obvious that the Fall of 1860 brought a definite cleavage and the American foundation at Williamsburg ceased to rely either for subjects or finances on the Ratisbon Motherhouse.

---

5. Crawford, *op. cit.,* Appendix, p. 368.
6. Kohler, Sister Mary Hortense, p. 46.

CHAPTER X

"By their fruits you will know them."
(Matthew 7:16)

When the dust raised by the furor of the events of 1860 began to settle, Mother Josepha was observed following her serene way, the quiet routine of daily religious life. It never occurred to Mother to question the legality of leaving the enclosure to teach the students in the adjoining building. Her years as teacher in Ratisbon where before her entrance into the community, civil authorities had forced the Sisters to assume the responsibility of teaching in the attached school, had been a sufficient apprenticeship.

There is little doubt, however, that the dichotomy between cloistered Second Order religious and the apostolic works of teaching and caring for orphans caused uneasiness in the sincere soul of Mother Josepha. The difficulties created by their dual role have been aptly described in "All the Way Is Heaven" by Katherine Burton:

> "As Second Order Dominicans, teaching was not the work they should be carrying on indefinitely. They taught from necessity. When they were at home in their own convent, they lived behind the grille, but there was a certain illogic in the fact that they went out to teach school and yet received their visitors in the convent only behind the grille.
>
> After long hours of teaching and saying the Divine Office, they did their housework at night or sometimes rose long before dawn to do the laundry in order to find time in their crowded day for both chanting the Office and teaching."[1]

It was long after the gentle Mother Josepha had passed away before this impossible situation was rectified. Under the leadership of Bishop Charles E. McDonnell, second Bishop of Brooklyn, and Mother Antonine the status of the community was changed in 1895 to that of the Third Order.

Sacrifices, patiently accepted by His followers, inevitably bring down the Divine favor. The edifying lives of Mother Josepha and her companions attracted the attention and won the admiration of several young women. One of them has the distinction of being the first postulant to present herself to the wise guidance

---

1. Burton, Katherine, *All the Way Is Heaven*, pp. 41-43.

of Mother Josepha. Margaret Bosslet, German born, was a domestic in Holy Trinity Parish. In March 1857 she asked for admittance to Holy Cross at the age of 22. It is important to recall the circumstances under which the Sisters lived and labored to appreciate the motives behind Margaret's determination to be a member of the pioneering group. No material advantages drew her, for their small makeshift convent and educational facilities would have discouraged anyone with ulterior motives.

Mother Josepha accepted Margaret as her own heart rejoiced at this first sign of growth in alien soil. However, reception of the habit was delayed thirteen months. Mother Josepha, though eager to see their number increase, tested this first American recruit to guarantee the true worth of the vocation. What a joyous day April 9, 1858 must have been for the Mother as she clothed the new novice in the beloved Dominican habit. The newly-blessed chapel in the convent only months old was fittingly bedecked for the occasion and Mother Josepha bestowed the name Sister Rosa on Margaret. Thus Margaret Bosslet was the first rose to bloom on the thorny bush in Williamsburg.

With the coming of Mother Benedicta in October 1858, a second candidate joined the novice, Sister Rosa. Crescentia Traubinger, a child of fourteen, began her preparation for reception of the habit on October 21, 1858. Almost two years of intensive, although primitive (by our present standards) training ensued before Dominic's habit replaced her secular dress on

August 4, 1860. In this postulant's acceptance one can see evidence of the community's policy of accepting rather young girls, a custom inherited from Ratisbon. To our sophisticated society today, it may look like "robbing the cradle." However, these supposed children became the sturdy trunk from which sprang the many American branches of the Dominican Order.

By 1862 the number of candidates had swelled to seven for we read in Msgr. Crawford's book that one of the consolations of the closing years of Mother Josepha's life was: "On August 4, 1862, the people of the parish thronged to the ceremony of the reception of the vows of seven candidates. This impressive scene, together with Father May's preaching and the example of the Sisters, whom the people almost adored, brought a notable increase to the community."[2]

In the foregoing paragraph a name, hitherto not mentioned, appears. Reverend Michael May, a Ratisbon priest who came to Williamsburg on March 30, 1859, was appointed assistant to the aging pastor, Father Raffeiner. The latter was not long in discovering the tremendous potential of his young curate and, possibly at his recommendation, Father May was appointed by Bishop Loughlin "confessor" to the small Dominican Community on August 24, 1859. This term, "confessor," was one used in that day for an advisor in spiritual and temporal affairs to a community. Thus,

---

2. Crawford, Rt. Rev. Eugene J., *Daughters of Dominic on Long Island* (Benziger, 1937), p. 96.

there was placed "a man of broad vision, unusual business ability, dogged perseverance and fatherly tenderness,"[3] at the beck and call of Mother Josepha. How Divine Providence foresaw the coming years that would try the soul of His valiant handmaid and gave her a bulwark of strength to uphold her.

While the internal life of the Community went along rather smoothly on its course, the external larger community of the country was undergoing an upheaval that almost brought about its collapse.

As far back as 1854, the Sisters as well as the priests were the butt of insults from the infamous "Know Nothing Party." In fact, the organization had waxed so bold as to organize mobs to harass the Church and led by a ruffian called Bill Poole, a march was formed at the volunteer firehouse against the Catholic Institutions of the city. The Sisters spent several hours of fearful expectancy when word reached Father Raffeiner that the group was headed for Holy Trinity parish buildings. By the time they reached Montrose Avenue, Father Raffeiner had encircled the parish plant with stalwart male parishioners and the mob was stopped in its tracks at the sight of the determined old priest and his small army. Periodically, these threats were renewed for the next six years and rumblings of the larger conflict to come were heard in the small community in Williamsburg. By 1861, with the firing on Fort Sumter, the country was torn

---

3. *Ibid.,* p. 92.

asunder and brother faced brother across the firing line.

Brooklyn did not escape the impact of the war and members of Holy Trinity parish were quick to enter the ranks of combatants. Mother Josepha's heart was torn as news of the bloody battles seeped into the cloister through the children in the school. Some of their fathers had already paid the supreme sacrifice for their country, and it is not improbable to suppose that the idea of a place set aside for orphans and neglected children should have been conceived at this time.

Her love for children, particularly orphaned children, prompted her to cooperate with Father May in establishing an Orphan Home Society for the care of orphaned and neglected children of the parish. The first little convent, Mr. Gunther's house, was offered to the Society to house the children by the Sisters and they undertook the added burden along with their other works for God's glory.

During this trying time, the progress of the school continued undiminished; the Sisters worked energetically with their apt students. If four years previously, 1856, this commendation could appear in the "katholische Kirchen-Zeitung" of New York:

"I must at once observe on this occasion that the Sisters of St. Dominic (from the Mother-House of Regensburg) in the three years of their stay here, have already acquired great merits in the education and training of youth and are continuously working for the great blessing of the parish."[4]

how much more so would the four following years 1856-1860 have deserved additional praise.

Divine Providence chose this time of tranquillity within and turmoil without revealing to Mother Josepha that Calvary's height would soon be reached where her final crucifixion would culminate her steady ascent up its steep sides. Although Mother Josepha was frail in appearance, there is no indication at the time of her acceptance as a candidate by Holy Cross that she lacked good health. Msgr. Crawford declares:

"Accompanying these documents, and others giving her qualifications as a teacher, ... is a health certificate stating that although Teresa Witzlhofer was slender there was no inclination to tuberculosis. Her ancestors on both sides were farmers, indicating a rugged family strain."[5]

The living conditions to which the Sisters were subjected during that first winter of 1853-1854 were sufficiently rugged to defy even the most robust to survive.

"It was not until the beginning of the year 1854,

---

4. *Katholische Kirchen-Zeitung,* Thurs., May 22, 1856. (New York, "Philos" (Correspondent).

5. Crawford, *op. cit.,* p. 100.

after four months of living in the cramped quarters of the rectory basement that a new arrangement was made for the Sisters. They were offered a part of the school, the basement of the old church, as a convent. . . . but physically the new home, if such it could be called, was less satisfactory than the former. Even protection from the elements was lacking—the cracked and dilapidated walls let the rain and snow into the very beds of the Sisters."[6]

Sister Josepha, along with her three companions suffered severely during that first winter. One of them, Sister Francesca, developed tuberculosis dying a year later. Mother Josepha did not spare herself, refusing to ask anyone to do what she herself did not do. Being a true Mother, her ministrations to her dying daughter, Francesca, coupled with the long hours of work and concern for her small group furrowed the soil for the seeds of tuberculosis in her own lungs.

For nine years, Mother Josepha continued her labors and bore the crosses of misunderstanding and loneliness while her health declined. She had to accept the demand of her dear first companion, Sister Augustine, for separation from Williamsburg and independence for the Second Street foundation in 1861. It is difficult to grasp the reasons behind the request as distance here was no problem. It clearly indicates at this time that Sister Augustine recognized Mother Josepha as Prioress with power to grant such a separa-

6. Crawford, *op. cit.,* p. 66.

tion. It was not, however, until 1869 that the formal separation was accomplished, five years after Mother Josepha's death.

Despite the ravages of the disease, Mother Josepha's spirit remained dauntless and the gentle Prioress found in the energetic new pastor, Father May, who had succeeded Father Raffeiner at his death on July 16, 1861, a tower of strength.

Mother's first capitulation to ill health came in her resignation as principal of the school. Sister Seraphina Staimer, the strong, young Sister who joined the group in 1855 took over the running of the expanding school. Mother remained, however, a teacher par excellence and continued to instruct a few of the older girls in the convent in the arts that labeled one a well-trained young lady. These included painting, embroidery and the making of wax flowers — arts in which Mother Josepha excelled.

It is a tantalizing problem to find no portrait or likeness of the woman who built better than she knew. One must be satisfied with a word portrait drawn by two reliable witnesses. Mother Catherine, Prioress of the Community from 1901 to 1913, attended the school conducted by the Sisters. She speaks of "the noble bearing of the tall gentle Mother who was so patient and wax-like, similar to a lily drooping on its stem."[7] She would gaze rapturously at the lovely lady who would reward the gaze with her beautiful smile.

---

7. Crawford, *op. cit.*, p. 95.

A future Mistress of Novices and Council member, Mother Philomena, at a tender, impressionable age stole sly glances through the picket fence surrounding the convent garden "at the tall, stately Mother resting herself in the garden."[8]

From these two accounts, each must be content to fill out mentally the appearance of our dear Foundress and each will bring to the task her own special insights to discover for herself a woman worthy of her loving gratitude for laying the foundation on which her own vocation rests so solidly.

By 1862 Mother Josepha, wracked with pain, her endless nights broken by hacking coughing and drenching fever, was wasting away. She was to suffer two excruciating years before death would release her. On August 21, 1862, Maria Josepha Witzlhofer sold her share of the Motherhouse property equal to one thousand dollars to Maria Seraphine Staimer, Maria Emilia Barth, Maria Augustine Neuhierl and Maria Cunigunda Schell.

This extract in the Motherhouse archives reveals the manner in which property was bought, maintained and sold in the names of the pioneer Sisters. This posed a serious danger to the welfare of the Community, since relatives of a deceased Sister could claim the Sister's share of the Community's property. Fortunately, Father May, with his shrewd business sense, terminated this precarious situation by advising the Sisters to incorporate the Community. Legal steps

---

8. Crawford, *op. cit.*, p. 95.

were taken and four years after Mother Josepha's death this legal document was drawn up:

"First: The corporate name of the society hereby organized is to be 'The Nuns of the Order of St. Dominic of the City of Brooklyn, New York.

❋ ❋ ❋

Third: The affairs of the corporation shall be managed by Five Managers or Directors and the following persons shall be Managers or Directors for the first year and until others shall be elected in their place, viz. Mary Seraphine Staimer, Mary Augustine Neuhierl, Mary Emilia Barth, Mary Cunigunda Schell, Mary Aloysia Fucks.

❋ ❋ ❋

Witness our hands and seals the twenty-third day of May 1868.

> Signed and sealed in the presence of Jacob Zimmer"[9]

Late in 1862, Mother Josepha turned over the supervision of the small community to her young assistant, Sister Seraphine, whose love and admiration for her ailing Prioress is evident in this excerpt from her diary:

"She it was who by her indomitable patience and

9. Crawford, *op. cit.*, p. 112.

holy prudence under all kinds of miserable circumstances and endless troubles saved the little community from foundering in those early years. In her, our community surely has an intercessor in Heaven and I ascribe to her prayers the rapid development of our convent and the singular blessing of God which it enjoys."[10]

Death was slow in coming and Mother Josepha spent the days in patient suffering encouraging by her loving interest the apostolic labors of her community. Frequently, she could be seen resting in the small convent garden.

Before she herself was called to face her Judge, two young members of the community succumbed to the same all-too-prevalent disease, tuberculosis. Her namesake, Sister Josepha, only fifteen years old, made her profession on her deathbed on December 21, 1863, the youngest professed Sister in the community. Only seven days passed before the next victim, Sister Vincentia Bahr, 26 years of age, was found dead.

Finally, the Divine Mercy took compassion on the frail invalid and Mother Josepha stepped into the Eternal Embrace surely with the words of welcome to the faithful steward:

"Well done, good and faithful servant; because thou hast been faithful over a few things, I will

---

10. Crawford, *op. cit.,* p. 101.

set thee over many; enter into the joy of thy master." (Matt. 25:23)

Mother was forty-six years old and lacking only one year to celebrating her silver jubilee of profession.

Her body, dressed in the simple Dominican habit she wore with such grace, was brought from the convent to the church where her faithful co-worker, Father May, celebrated the Mass. Then interment was made in Holy Trinity Cemetery until 1896 when the remains were carried to the Novitiate Cemetery and interred in the tomb reserved for deceased Mother Prioresses of the Community.

Msgr. Crawford in his history of the Community summarizes briefly the qualities that marked Mother Josepha as a woman of whom the Community may well be proud:

"Her sterling worth makes her limitations very small indeed. By her example she bequeathed her spiritual daughters the following great virtues:

1. Obedience to the Bishop and his representatives as the voice of the Vicar of Christ.
2. A wonderful perseverance in the face of disheartening obstacles. The spirit of this sorely tried woman was never broken.
3. A proper technical training for the various works of the Community. She was a highly talented woman and a very capable teacher.
4. Mother Josepha was the embodiment of

refinement and religious decorum, a woman of prayer and sacrifice. Although she tolerated a canonical looseness of administration because conditions made it necessary, she held to the observance of her Holy Rule and of the holy traditions of the Dominican Order most zealously. She bequeathed as a great heritage the custom of revering the Dominican Rule and unwritten traditions, which has been distinctive of the Community."[11]

11. Crawford, *op. cit.,* p. 100.

CHAPTER XI

"... like a grain of mustard seed ... the smallest of all the seeds; but when it grows up it is larger than any herb and becomes a tree, so that the birds of the air come and dwell in its branches."
(Matt. 13-31, 32)

Persons who have had a close call with "Sister Death" have been known to state that flashes of their whole life have instantaneously passed before their mind's eye. Could Mother Josepha's wildest dreams have embraced the panorama of Dominic's daughters stepping across the limiting borders of Brooklyn to leave their mark on practically every state of this vast Union.

Her death, ironically, occurred just as this Union was locked in a death struggle for its own survival. Only from heaven's ramparts could she behold the unfolding drama as shoot after shoot sprang from the weak sapling she had so patiently nourished during those eleven years.

Providence had given Mother Josepha a faithful young woman as companion in her declining years, and true to her commitment, Sister Seraphine took the reins dropped from the hand of Mother Josepha at the command of her Ordinary, Bishop Loughlin. With energy and courage she carried the small community forward for twenty-five years. She admits that the sudden increase in applicants to the Holy Cross Convent was due to the sufferings and prayers of her saintly predecessor. The Community totaled nine members at her accession and three hundred at her death; it had two houses, Holy Cross and Second Street in 1864 and over twenty stretching as far West as California in 1889 when Mother Seraphine died at the age of fifty-nine.

Just before the turn of the century, when change was in the air, and the death of the last of the pioneer Mothers had severed ties completely with Ratisbon, God raised to the office of Prioress, Mother Antonine, destined to be a cross bearer like her holy Foundress. Too, the diocese had a new bishop, Charles E. McDonnell, who "desired to set all things aright according to Canon Law."[1]

The Sisters had lost contact with the Dominican Order; they were partly Second Order in their reli-

---

1. Crawford, Rt. Rev. Eugene J., *Daughters of Dominic on Long Island* (Benziger, 1937), p. 145.

gious observances and partly Third Order in their active apostolate which now included teaching, the care of orphans and the nursing of the sick. Bishop McDonnell's first step was to query Bishop von Synestry as to the status of the Community of Dominican Sisters in his diocese. Paucity of documentary material and the death of all persons involved in the early history of the Community made the effort of the Bishop more difficult.

Finally, he requested his secretary, Reverend Geoge W. Mundelein, and the Sisters' spiritual director, Reverend John F. Hoffman, to investigate the Rule of the Third Order of Dominican Sisters of Stone, England. The two men adopted it to the circumstances of the Brooklyn Sisters and after a year's trial, the Bishop decreed that the Community should live according to the new Rule and Constitutions. Thus, the change from the Second to the Third Order was smoothly effected, and in 1895 the Community became diocesan in outlook and scope.

By the year 1910, the missionary aspect of the Community had disappeared and it in turn looked for fields afar to challenge its apostolic zeal. The expansion into the missions was accomplished by Mother Catherine Herbert. Puerto Rico received the first Dominicans from Brooklyn on August 20, 1910, growing over the years to nine houses including the Catholic University of Puerto Rico.

Tracing the Community's intricate spreading into other areas of this vast country can be accomplished best by a glance at the diagram found on page vii. Either directly or indirectly Holy Cross Convent, Brooklyn, has touched the lives of millions of American youth on every level of education. It likewise influenced through its numerous apostolic endeavors including schools, hospitals, homes for the aged, lay retreat work, summer camps, social work of all kinds, souls throughout the length and breadth of this land which felt ever so slightly the footsteps of the four pioneers on its shores in August 1853.

Proper training of the newcomers to the Community has always been one of the chief concerns of the Mothers from the Foundress to the present. Mother Seraphine seeing the need almost immediately, purchased a piece of property in Suffolk County and built the Novitiate of the Queen of the Holy Rosary on Albany Avenue, Amityville. Here, in the quiet of the countryside, a perfect replica of Ratisbon Motherhouse was completed in 1876.

During Mother Anselma's term of office, 1943-1955, as the neighborhood surrounding the original Motherhouse on Montrose and Graham Avenues deteriorated, she moved the center of the Community to Amityville.

Finally, Mother Bernadette de Lourdes, mindful of the Church's desire that young aspirants be fully trained spiritually and professionally before assuming their apostolate, built the present new Novitiate adjoining the original building.

Today, 1970, when space has been conquered and the moon invaded by man, the unassuming Mother

Josepha, claiming but a tiny piece of Community Cemetery, may well look back at the amazing growth of her small planting and echo the words of one of the Church's greatest missionaries, Paul,

> "I have planted, Apollos watered, but God has given the growth" (1 Cor. 3:6, 7).